No Longer Bound

Breaking Free from the Weight of Abandonment,
Child Sexual Abuse and Sexual Assault

Monaye Etana

B.O.Y. Publications, Inc.
c/o Author Copyrights
P.O. Box 1012
Lowell, NC 28098
www.alwaysbetonyourself.com

ISBN: 978-1-955605-06-9

Cover Design and Interior Design: B.O.Y. Enterprises, Inc.

Printed in the United States.

This book is dedicated to:

The inner child that still resides within us all.
Tony and Kaelyn, my dynamic duo. You have made me so proud.
Ruth and Bea for pouring into me.

Acknowledgments

The ability to bring a vision to life is not as simple as one may think. There are countless contributors who lend their invaluable skills, time, and support to help birth a book. When I say that I could not have done it without you all, I really mean it.

First and foremost, I have to thank my heavenly Father for carrying me throughout this process. It is only because of who He has been in my life, that I was able to share my journey to freedom with you. I am forever grateful for His love.

Shannon Wilkerson, you are the one who helped me to put my foot on the gas pedal. When I came to you with my vision, you understood why it was so important to me. You guided and supported me along the way. I can't thank you enough. A manuscript is nothing without an editor. Marvin Wilson Jr., your ability to make corrections while keeping the reader in mind is phenomenal. I really appreciate your patience and dedication. I also have to thank Otescia Johnson, for your formatting and book design expertise. Thank you for your hard work and professionalism on this project.

To my sister and stylist Lashawndra Storr, of Adorn by L, you were the first one to read over the initial draft and provide honest feedback. You encouraged me to keep going. When it came to my look, you knew how to put me together. I'll love you always. To my hairstylist Tea, you are the truth. I'd also like to thank my makeup artist, Jontrice Robinson for my natural beat. You definitely worked your magic. A huge thanks is in order to Anthony and Hannah Jenkins, of Greater Entertainment LLC for capturing my images. You guys are the best!

I am so very thankful to my friends and family who pushed and encouraged me to finish the book. I love you all. Reshon, I'm so blessed to have you as a friend. Thanks for listening, uplifting, and praying for me. Lastly, to my son and daughter Tony and Kaelyn, you are my world. Thank you for believing in me.

Table of Contents

Foreword

Abandonment, Abuse, Assault

Ugly words that describe ugly life changing experiences that leave a lingering residue, that for most, are difficult to overcome. These types of experiences shape who we are and how we engage with the rest of the world. They can make us more aware of physical and emotional dangers, which can keep us safe. However, they can also cause us to be less trusting and less capable of developing quality relationships with others. We may keep a safe, emotional distance from the people that we love as a defense mechanism and we may also hold loved ones closer than what is considered normal, as a way of protecting them from being victimized.

The trauma of these horrible experiences does not end when the act does. The confusion, pain, and heartache of it all, stays with us and requires healing. Though the act may have happened quickly, the healing part can be slow. It is a process that will require that you be patient, as well as love and be committed to yourself. As we begin to heal from these violations, we can see improvement in the way that we experience life. Our relationships can be more fulfilling, we may feel less vulnerable and more in control, and we may enjoy life with renewed freedom.

The thing about trauma, is that though we will all go through various phases of healing, it will not look the same for all of us. Two people can experience the exact same traumatic event and their healing process and journey to freedom, can be completely different. In this book, you get an inside look at the journey of one woman navigating her way through abandonment, child sexual abuse and assault, and what healing was like for her. Though your story may be different, you will be able to relate to many things shared and hopefully be inspired to embark on your own mission to remove the chains of your past. In some way you will grow from this story and hopefully be able to turn the page on trauma, entering into a place of being no longer bound.

As you read this very real and raw account of the Author's past, it may trigger emotions that had been previously suppressed. She has exposed the dark places and unpacked the things that many of us carry with us but keep quiet about. This level of transparency was birthed from a desire to set others free. I encourage you to allow yourself to process all of those emotions and journey through with her. Reflect on your personal story and how you will grow from it in order to experience restoration. It is truly the best thing that you could do for yourself. This process may be hard, but necessary and worth it. Know that people are rooting for you, praying for you and that there is a great life on the other side of trauma.

Shannon Wilkerson

Introduction

Rising Above It All

"You may write me down in history with your bitter, twisted lies, you may trod me in the very dirt but still, like dust, I'll rise."

These powerful words, written by the incomparable Maya Angelou would unknowingly become the theme for my life. And Still I Rise. Four words that must have been deeply imbedded on the inside of me from the moment I took my first breath. A life that would soon be filled with unexpected pain and devastation which would continue throughout my adult years. In this book, I want to share an authentic account of what courage, perseverance, and the resolve to survive encompassed for me.

As you take this butterfly journey with me on my path to self- love, rediscovery, and joy, you may experience a range of emotions. Allow yourself to feel them all. It is my hope that in some way, that you are encouraged to discover your own road to freedom.

Part I- The Caterpillar

Abandonment

"The LORD Himself goes before you and will be with you; He will never leave you nor forsake you. Do not be afraid; do not be discouraged."
-Deuteronomy 31:8 (NIV)

You may say, I know what abandonment is and I am sure that you do. Many times, we can see how others have been impacted by something, but we may not see it within ourselves. I want to show you how to recognize the signs because it is possible that it may have been present in your life or someone close to you. Once we have identified the signs, we can take on the task of working towards overcoming those obstacles. We all have the need for healthy connections and development, but when those needs are unmet, we can develop feelings of abandonment. Although there are several forms of abandonment, I will focus on three of them in the next few chapters — physical, emotional, and abandonment of self.

Chapter One

Unexpected Departures

P hysical abandonment can occur when a person intentionally leaves you. For a child, it can stem from the loss of a parent through death or divorce. Other ways that children can be affected include having parents who are dealing with an addiction, parents that are depressed and emotionally unavailable, and children who are often home alone. This can cause trauma that we may not recognize until later in life. Physical abandonment can also result from a breakup, divorce, or the end of a close friendship. Adults who have experienced this type of abandonment may have trust issues, be controlling, be a people pleaser or find themselves envious of other relationships.

Have you ever lost someone and wondered why they left? Or if you could have done anything to stop him or her from leaving? I have certainly had those types of thoughts. Although they are normal, they do not contribute to our overall well-being. Instead, it causes us to question our self-worth, increases the risk of anxiety, depression, emotional eating, or the development of other coping mechanisms. Thinking back over your life, have you often found yourself feeling jealous of others, being clingy in relationships or finding it hard to keep connections with friends because you wanted to keep them from getting too close? Or maybe you found yourself being emotionally unavailable and unable to commit because deep down inside, you wanted to protect yourself.

We may tell ourselves, that if we keep our walls up and that person leaves us, we cannot get hurt. I cannot tell you the number of times that I have experienced these exact feelings! Unfortunately, all of this is rooted in abandonment and fear. Fear holds us back from being our true selves. It can be so strong that it prevents us from living our dreams, stepping outside of our comfort zone, advancing in our careers, or even crossing something off of our bucket list. These feelings can be so intense that they can also push the people that we love and care about away from us. Fear of abandonment can be paralyzing if we let it. Do you know what can push us forward? Faith

> *Fear holds us back from being our true selves.*

My feelings of abandonment started as a young child. I was three years old and most likely looking forward to turning four within a few days. Unfortunately, my life would change dramatically within that time frame. My mother who was 21 years old and married to my father, committed suicide. In thinking back to the circumstances surrounding her death, I can only imagine what her state of mind was. I wonder if she felt empty, worthless, angry, and alone. No one will truly know how she felt, but sadly, she saw suicide as her only option.

The loss of my mother deeply impacted all who knew her. She was well liked and respected on her job, and she had many friends. She loved to cook and dance! (Maybe this is where I got it from.) I cannot imagine the pain that my father experienced. Although they married young, it was true love. He loved her immensely. I can remember him crying while playing records in the house that we lived in at the time. I can only imagine the memories that he must have been reflecting on. When I look back at old pictures, they looked happy. Her death was also extremely tough for my uncles since my mother was their only sister. My grandmother was so heartbroken that she could not attend the funeral and was prescribed medication for anxiety and depression. I don't think her heart ever fully healed from the loss of her precious baby girl, but I'll always admire her strength. For me, the questions came as I got older. I wondered why my mother had left me. I mean, didn't she love me? How could she leave her children? Didn't she want to be around for all of the milestone moments? Who would teach me all of the things that girls need to know? To lose my mom; the woman who brought me into this world was something that would impact me in ways that I would not understand until years later.

After my mother passed away, me and my then one- year old sister were cared for by both sets of our grandparents for the next few years. My father did his best with trying to cope with the loss of the woman he had been high school sweethearts with while still trying to provide for two young girls. He has always been a man full of strength and determination which I admire. Although my grandparents loved and spoiled us just as most grandparents do, I remember feeling sad sometimes when I was by myself. I had great friends in the neighborhood, I went to Sunday school and church, I was a Girl Scout and I wanted for nothing tangible, but I wanted my mother.

Eventually my father remarried when I was around seven years old, and we moved into a new home. I experienced additional feelings of abandonment but more on a level of anxiety because this was new to me. This meant that I would not get to see my grandparents every day like I was used to. We had so many great times, and the bond with them could never be replaced. There were so many thoughts and questions that ran through my mind. What will my stepmom be like? Do I have to call her mom? Since she had no kids of her own, would she like me?

Imagine going from two homes where you felt nothing but love, to a new environment where you were unsure of how you would be received. My stepmom was young, and she also had to adjust to a new way of life with a new husband and two kids. Were things smooth right away? No, there was definitely an adjustment period that had to occur over the years. Having to adapt to a blended family can create challenges for everyone involved. I not only had a new mom, but new cousins, aunties and uncles, and a new grandmother. The level of uncertainty that I felt was unexplainable. In my young mind, I was being removed from my "safe house" with my grandparents and hoping that my new family would accept me. There were moments where I also wondered if I got use to them, would they leave me too?

According to the Mayo Clinic, it can take years or even longer for a child to really adjust to a new stepfamily. In many cases, family counseling is helpful. Sometimes, children experience feelings such as:

- Being uncomfortable in new surroundings
- Feeling excluded
- Torn between the new family and the old
- Alone in dealing with feelings
- Being disciplined by only the step- parent

I know that we would have benefitted from having some family therapy sessions. Unfortunately, it has always been frowned upon within the black community. I am not sure that my parents even knew that we needed counseling. It is possible that they were only parenting based on what they saw growing up. Cycles tend to repeat over and over again. As a young child and throughout my teenage years, reading and music became my coping mechanisms. I would lose myself in the stories of fiction or let the music that I listened to create the feelings of euphoria that were absent in my life. The first novel that I remember being immersed in was, "Where the Red Fern Grows". It was about the love between a boy and his dog. If you have ever had a pet, then you know that they love their owners unconditionally. I wonder if the desire for that type of love is what drew me to that particular book. Later in life, I would develop other ways to cope with my pain.

> ***It is possible that they were only parenting based on what they saw growing up.***

From middle school through high school, I was a shy, awkward, and insecure girl. While I had some good experiences such as my time spent playing the clarinet, singing in the chorus, being on the ROTC drill team, and winning the Jr. High school pageant, there were also less than favorable experiences. I wasn't a part of the popular crew and I recall being teased about certain things that I wore to school. One day in particular, I overheard a group of girls giggling about what I had on that day. I couldn't understand why people were so mean spirited. When I got home from school, I cried. I was hurt and angry. Why didn't people like me? I was always nice and considerate of others.

On top of dealing with my issues at school and trying to make the best of my home life, I experienced another loss in my life when my grandaddy R.C. died. He always showed me unconditional love. I was his sugar baby as he called me. We went fishing together, he would take me to the candy store, we picked up sugar cane and I'd always enjoy riding in the back of his station wagon everywhere we went. He even taught me how to get all of the meat off of a neckbone! I will never forget one of his birthdays where we put on Stevie Wonder's version of Happy birthday and sang to him. He cried so many tears of joy that day. Now, don't get me wrong, I know that my father loved me, but he was more of a provider and often worked at night. Here I was once again, left trying to understand why people that were supposed to love me kept leaving me. All I wanted was to feel valued and needed. While I had a family that provided the everyday necessities of life, the little girl inside of me wanted, no needed more. I needed to be affirmed, reassured, and heard, but because these things were missing, my voice could not be found. Everything that I wanted to verbalize about my feelings stayed on the inside of me. I often wondered what was wrong with me.

Why do we do this? We internalize things as if we are the cause of them which is so far from the truth. As children, we can only see so far which is based on our limited view of the real world. So, when someone leaves our life, those experiences become truth in our eyes. We teach ourselves that we cannot depend on anyone to be there for us, or we are unworthy. If we are not able to look deeply into our feelings, we could very well grow up with some beliefs that are untrue. When someone leaves us as children, we are not to blame. These experiences early on in my life added to my feelings of inadequacy throughout my life. I knew that I was destined for something great, but I was not sure if I had what it took to get there. I had a roof over my head, clothes to wear, food to eat, and attended regular church services but I still felt incomplete.

Your situation may have been completely different than mine. It is possible that you are unable to point out any particular life event that left you feeling abandoned and that's okay. It does not negate your feelings in any way. Regardless of when and how your abandonment issues started, the key is to not allow them to control your life. Do I still have abandonment triggers? Sure. But what I have realized is that people are imperfectly human. Whether it was intentional abandonment as it occurred with my mom or unintentional as it occurred with my grandfather, I chose not to get lost in the "what ifs." I can never change my past, but I can learn and grow from it. My value and self-worth were not determined by those that left me. Coming to that realization took some real work and it did not happen overnight, do you hear me? Some days are easier than others, but my future lies ahead.

I have been where you may be right now in your life. Whether you have felt abandoned by the loss of your husband, boyfriend, child, or family member, it is indeed a real feeling. I would never want you to ignore your feelings because they are valid. While all loss isn't the same, the loss of something or someone that we cherished needs to be addressed. Loss leads to grief. As a certified Grief Recovery Method Specialist, I have helped people acknowledge their pain and face it head on. It is perfectly okay to grieve what you lost or never had. Just because you are in a period of grieving, does not make you weak. For many of us, the child inside of us never got the chance to grieve. You hold the key to your own recovery. There is help available, but the first step is yours to take. You do not have to remain stuck.

One thing I also know, is that God, my Creator loves me no matter what. His love is unchanging, faithful, and comforts us in times of need. Psalm 136:26 says, "Give thanks to the God of heaven, for His steadfast love endures forever." Regardless of who stays or goes, He is with us always. Don't you know whose you are? You are a child of the KING! You may feel like you have lost your crown, but it is still there.

> **When someone leaves us, we are not to blame.**

Recovering from abandonment is not easy. The trauma we experience can show up in many areas of our lives. We look to other people to make us feel good about ourselves. In addition, we can become codependent and needy. All of our power is basically given away. In a way, it is like abandoning ourselves. If everyone else that loved me left, why should I care about myself? You should care about yourself because you are worth it. You were created for greatness. People that you may not have even met yet need you. Reclaiming your power is a process but it is necessary to lose the victim mentality and start walking in victory. Pick up your crown and wear it proudly.

SELF REFLECTIONS

What can you do to start living a life that you love and stop depending on others for validation? Ask yourself these questions and take action.

1. **Where did your abandonment issues come from? (Childhood or a previous relationship)**

   _____

   _____

   _____

   _____

   _____

   _____

2. **Have you done anything to address your feelings?**

   _____

   _____

   _____

   _____

3. **What do you say to yourself when you look in the mirror? Are the words positive or negative?**

   _____

   _____

   _____

   _____

   _____

4. Have you positively affirmed yourself today? Write down
   positive affirmations every day using the words I AM.
   (example: I am strong)

_____

_____

_____

_____

_____

_____

_____

_____

_____

_____

_____

_____

_____

_____

Chapter Two

The Well Runs Deep

When I think about thoughts and emotions, I know that they can cover a wide range from happiness to sadness, anger, doubt, loneliness, or insignificance. Emotional abandonment is a state of feeling unwanted, unloved, or unimportant by someone you care about. It may occur in many situations that we are completely unaware of. We can have everything else going okay in our lives but feel like something is missing. Do you know what I mean? Work life is fine, our relationships are fine, our health is fine, but there is a feeling that we just can't shake. A wife may feel emotionally abandoned by her husband because he is a workaholic. Or maybe there are addictions to other things outside of the relationship like gambling or sports that take time away from her. Maybe your friendships with girlfriends or family members have changed.

As a child, maybe you were not allowed to express yourself or there was little communication. You may have been raised in a household where you learned that your feelings were not important. Parents often tell their kids to do what they are told with no questions asked. In my opinion, this robs a child of their need to feel validated and heard. This teaches them that what they say is of no value to anyone. I am sure that you know someone that had this experience growing up if it wasn't you.

Everyone has their own individual needs, but these are the most basic:

- To feel valued
- To be appreciated
- To be nurtured
- To be heard
- Understood by others
- Love and affection
- Quality time

This seems easy enough, right? Unfortunately, we are not going to get every need met in a relationship nor should we expect it. It is not the responsibility of your significant other to be everything to you. When you expect them to do that, you leave yourself open for disappointment. Of course, your partner should support you and be there to comfort you, but you must take ownership of what you are feeling. Until you are healed, you will continue to abandon yourself to prevent the abandonment by others. There will be people and things that ignite your triggers, but the key is to figure out how to not let them get the best of you.

I remember dating a guy for a while and we had great chemistry. We did many things together. He was fun, spontaneous, surprised me with gifts, had good morals and he was fine fine! (I had to say that twice.) He would always listen to me and gave good advice. At some point, his role changed at his job, and this required him to devote more time to working. I understood this of course since I had my own career. However, over time our relationship became strained.

We talked less. We saw each other less. If plans were made, either they fell through, or the vibe between us was different. He told me that it was due to job stress and while I knew what he was going through, my issues with abandonment caused me to jump to conclusions. I feared that he was no longer interested in me the way that he was before, and that he would end the relationship soon. So, what did I do? I broke things off with him first.

Looking back at that relationship and what I have learned since that time, I understand that I allowed my fears to take over. The lack of communication between us and me feeling ignored led to resentment. Have you ever dealt with these feelings in a relationship? Instead of making my concerns known, I talked to my friends about it. I mean, that is what friends are for right?

> *Until you are healed, you will continue to abandon yourself to prevent the abandonment by others.*

The truth about emotional abandonment is that we do not realize how deep it runs. I believe that I would have handled that situation differently if I did not have a fear of abandonment. The issue with fear is that it will show up in the present even if the person you are with has no intention of abandoning you. How do you think he felt? Confused? Misunderstood? Rejected? I am quite sure it was one or all of those things.

The first thing that I should have done was a self-assessment. I should have asked myself, what are my needs? If I don't understand my needs, how can I explain them to anyone else? The next thing would be to have a conversation with him to communicate what those needs are. You may be thinking, he should know what is wrong! However, we know that's impossible because people are not mind readers.

During your conversation, be honest about how you feel when things are said or are not said. Tune into how you really feel and work together to come up with a solution. Make a commitment to tap into each other on a regular basis in order to keep the lines of communication open.

Being able to recognize the signs of abandonment is key.

- Recognize the signs — jealousy, clinginess, aggressiveness, thinking the worst
- Determine where it started
- Was it emotional or physical or both?
- Identify your triggers
- Accept your responsibility with the issue
- Think before reacting
- Do not be afraid to discuss your feelings
- Resist the need to be perfect
- Evaluate how you handle rejection

When we have death of a relationship from someone that we loved, it hurts. Regardless of who initiated the breakup or whether it was mutual, there is a process that most people go through. The end of a relationship often throws us into a grieving process. You may be thinking but no one actually died so how is it grief? As I mentioned before, loss has many forms. The time that we spend with the other person, creating memories, the constant communication and effort given, creates a bond between the couple. Depending on how long the relationship lasted, we get very accustomed to having that person in our lives. So, when the relationship ends, our hearts yearn and ache for what use to be. We are experiencing a true loss in our lives. It's normal to miss what was lost and the effects will vary from person to person. There isn't a set amount of time for experiencing any of these emotions either. The most common thing that people seek is closure but what is truly needed is the completion of our grief. In other words, we need to deal with the unfinished portion of that relationship. If we don't, we can end up living our lives in a place of regret. This can add to our feelings of emotional abandonment.

I know all too well what that feels like. I was in a relationship that was slowly failing, and it ended rather abruptly without me being able to gain closure in the way that I needed/wanted to. I was blindsided, angry, disgusted, and hurt. Because I was denied closure in the way that I sought it, it forced me to allow myself the time needed to go through every heartfelt emotion and once I came to terms with what my truth really was, my heart was able to heal. Pain will either push you forward or backwards. We must choose which direction we are going to go. Sometimes pain will even paralyze us. We can't find peace, we don't want to work, eat or talk to anyone. The only thing we look forward to is sleeping because then we don't have to deal with the pain. Unfortunately, this only keeps all of our emotions bottled up and it does nothing good for our overall health. Finding positive ways to deal with our feelings is critical. I had to really dig deep into my faith during that period. I started to journal from early on to release some of my feelings as well. Regardless of what methods you choose, make sure that they are positive ones.

The same way that our emotions can cause us to have anxiety in a situation over the thought of someone leaving, they can also cause us to keep everything inside. How many times have you been in a situation where after the fact you said to yourself, I should have said this or that? Many of us refrain from saying what we really think because we don't want to look stupid or be judged. We also create this false sense of ourselves in order to appear a certain way to others.

According to Psychologist Anne Wilson Schaef, "When we change ourselves to fit into a situation, we may be depriving that situation of the very element it needs to become what it can become." In other words, we could very well be the missing piece to the puzzle! Never allow anyone or anything to water you down. You are a worthy and unique woman who was made imperfectly perfect. Your laugh, style, personality, intellect, and quirks are like none other. Sometimes we can downplay just how valuable we are when we don't embrace our authenticity.

We all have something to contribute and whether you believe it or not, someone needs your gifts and talents. No one has the right to ask us to be a certain size, dress a certain way, or conform to their ideas of what is right. What you see is what you get, flaws and all and I refuse to lose myself in order to make someone else feel better. I wasn't put on this earth to please people, and neither were you. Living our lives in this way is unhealthy. It adds unnecessary stress and pressure which can lead to health issues or feeling overwhelmed because you cannot manage it all. We have to prioritize what is important, set healthy boundaries and be okay with our decisions.

Many of these lessons would have been so helpful in my younger days, but we live and learn, right? There are times when I reflect back at various moments throughout my life and literally shake my head. But despite it all, this once lost and cautious young girl grew into a confident, strong, and fierce overcomer of so many things. Every day I do my best to protect and maintain my peace. It's not always easy but it is vital in order to keep my sanity. Of course, there will always be something that tries to disturb those things, but we have the choice in what we accept into our space.

> **If we don't understand our needs, how can we explain them to anyone else?**

Finding ways to maintain our peace can be challenging but it's not impossible. With everything that we do on a daily basis, it can become a real task when trying to find time to unwind and reset. However, we have to show up for ourselves. It doesn't have to be anything that takes a lot of energy. Showing up for ourselves include the mental and physical aspects as well. Here are some things that we can incorporate into our lifestyle to help with protecting our peace:

- Commit to having daily "me" time — this can be your favorite cup of coffee, reading a few pages of a book, or a short stroll outside.
- Focus on only the important things — life can leave us with so much on our "to do lists" which can leave us frustrated and anxious. Do one thing at a time.

- Separate yourself from toxic people — who needs negativity in their life?
- Do things that you enjoy — take up a new interest or pamper yourself.
- Meditate and practice gratitude — make a list of what you are grateful for.
- Fuel your body with healthy foods and get exercise —you'll feel better while doing your body good.

In tough times we must remember that we are not alone. Deuteronomy 31:6 says, "Be strong and courageous, do not be afraid or tremble at them, for the Lord your God is the One who goes with you. He will not fail you or forsake you." Many times, strength comes from having courage. However, sometimes we don't feel like we can rely on our own strength. Guess what? We are not supposed to. Where our strength ends, God's will begin because His power is made perfect in our weakness. It is with Him that we are victorious.

> **Sometimes we can downplay just how valuable we are when we don't embrace our authenticity.**

SELF REFLECTIONS

We all need to take time to refocus and refresh our minds on the positive things through introspection. Ask yourself these questions.

1. **What things can I do to start making myself a priority?**

    _____

    _____

    _____

    _____

    _____

2. **Can I write down the negative ways that I cope with feelings of abandonment or anxiety? Jot down some positive alternatives.**

    _____

    _____

    _____

    _____

    _____

3. **Am I holding on to something that I need to let go of?**

    _____

    _____

    _____

    _____

    _____

4. **What makes me smile? Make a list of 15 things.**

1._____

2._____

3._____

4._____

5._____

6._____

7._____

8._____

9._____

10._____

11._____

12._____

13._____

14._____

15._____

Chapter Three

Your Needs Are Important

We live in a world where everyone is on the move, technology is constantly changing, and people are consumed with work, school, or the next hot topic. There are priorities and responsibilities that we must tend to whether that be deadlines, appointments, household needs, or caring for a loved one. They all take focus and commitment, and of course, time; however, they can leave us with little time to devote to our personal interests or talents that we possess.

How many times have you told yourself that you need to take up a hobby, or you would like to start on that project you have been putting off? Maybe you have things that you used to do but you put them on the back burner. There may be some of you that do not know what you really enjoy because you were never allowed to explore your interests. I will get back to that topic but let me explain why we need to have our own interests.

Each one of us are uniquely different and the things we like to do will vary as well. The great news is that the world is full of limitless activities for us to get involved in. It is important to have a hobby or an outlet as I like to call it, for many reasons. It allows us to find enjoyment in the things we are passionate about in our spare time. It can also be an opportunity to impact another person's life in a positive way if you decided to volunteer for example.

There are many advantages to exploring our personal interests:

- Having interests works wonders to relieve the stresses of day-to-day life. We can relax and enjoy other activities.
- They allow us to be able to share our interests and experiences with others.
- It expands our social lives and the opportunity to create bonds with new people.
- Developing new interests and using our talents can boost our confidence.
- It builds patience as we learn a new skill.
- As we take on a new activity, we gain knowledge while being challenged.

Regardless of what activities you are involved in, the key is to make sure it is something you enjoy. The more you enjoy it, the more you are likely to stick with it, while relieving stress and that is definitely a win!

Unfortunately, there are circumstances that may prevent the proper development of our interests. As parents, we want the best for our children. If the pregnancy goes as expected, we nurture them in our bellies for 9 months, while anxiously preparing for their arrival. We want every detail to be perfect from the type of baby clothes to the design of the baby's room. In our minds and hearts, we vow to protect them from anything or anyone that could cause harm. Sometimes in our efforts to be the best for our children, we can stunt their independence and self-confidence.

According to Psychology Today, at some point we should ask ourselves are we doing too much for them? Are we over-parenting and not giving them room to explore their own likes and dislikes? Many times, it is difficult for us parents to loosen the grasp and it becomes more about us than our children. Whether we try to put them in every activity possible or prevent them from doing anything extracurricular, these can be based on our own experiences growing up. As children grow from childhood to adolescence, they should have a voice not only in their own homes but also be respected for their own thoughts and opinions as human beings. Think back to your experiences growing up. Were you allowed to try out different things like art, sports, music, or taking up a craft? Were your interests considered? How do you think those experiences or lack of experiences impacted your life?

> **Sometimes in our efforts to be the best for our children, we can stunt their independence and self-confidence.**

Outside of what I already mentioned, I wasn't involved in many activities growing up. When the summertime came, my sister and I knew we would be going to Vacation Bible School which was held at the church we normally attended on Sundays. Vacation Bible School is a program offered by many churches which offers activities and educates children about God. For about two weeks, we would enjoy bible stories, prayer, games, and various other things to keep our interests. The church van would pick us up and bring us back home. Once summer was over and school resumed, I remember wanting to participate in extracurricular activities such as cheerleading, drama club and band. However, after school I had to come home to do homework and watch my younger siblings (by my dad and stepmom) and make sure whatever chores I was responsible for were done. I still have that overseer personality today.

Now don't get me wrong, every child should learn how to do chores. They help kids learn self-reliance and responsibility. It gives them a sense of confidence in being able to complete tasks and become independent. These are skills that will help them be successful in taking care of others as well as themselves in the future. Most kids hate doing chores unless they are rewarded for it. Wait, reward them for doing what they are supposed to be doing anyway? Yes! A reward does not automatically mean monetarily. According to Eugene Beresin M.D., if we are raised in a home that is grounded in validation, praise, and gratitude, that inadvertently gives an emotional reward which contributes to their well-being as mature and responsible people. I can't say that my home environment provided all of those things but having two grandparents to fill that void certainly helped a lot.

B-A-L-A-N-C-E. We all need it. Even children/teenagers. Without balance we can become overwhelmed with life's daily tasks and that leaves little room to enjoy all the joys of life. As mentioned in Children's Health, free time is necessary to relax and recharge. It is also during these times that they learn how to handle conflicts, be leaders, and explore with their minds. We also must make sure that once the children have given a specific interest a fair shot, we support their choice to continue or stop participating.

As women, we do it all. We wear many hats in the workplace, at home, at church, at school and often at the expense of our own sanity. If you look at your life, would you say that there is enough balance? There was a time in my life where I worked over 55 hours a week. The money was great, but I had no time for anything else that I wanted or needed to do. My kids had already left the home, so I didn't have the daily mom duties, but I still needed "me time" and had other family members that I didn't get to spend time with as much as I'd like.

After a certain point in time, I began to feel the consequences of working so much. I had anxiety, high stress, hair loss and I just hated what my life had turned into. In addition to my job, I was also involved in mentoring other women and serving in my church. I still don't know how I kept that up for so long. Eventually I had to make a decision to do what was best for me and my well-being. I quit that job! What good is it to make great money at the expense of what is important? That was a form of self-abandonment. Now I know some of us (myself included) are high achievers and feel like we have to be Superwoman. That is a learned behavior, and it usually stems from our upbringing.

In her blog, Happily Imperfect, Sharon Martin, LCSW says that we learn to do whatever is needed to avoid criticism, pain, conflict and physical or emotional pain. We suppress our true selves and feel that our worth is based on accomplishments or reaching a certain goal. Our personal interests then take a back seat to everything else.

Staying busy may be what keeps you going and that is fine but doing too much has its consequences and risks. We not only run the risk of personal burnout, but also declining health and changes in friendships and familial connections. We are so used to putting the needs of others before our own so the signs of self-abandonment might not be obvious. Do any of the following examples of self-abandonment look familiar to you?

Signs of self-abandonment:

- Refusing to speak up for yourself, allowing others to take advantage of you, not making your needs known.
- Doing things that do not support your personal values.
- Giving too much in relationships.
- Being critical or judgmental to yourself when you don't meet your standards of perfectionism.
- Putting the needs of others before your own needs.
- Hiding parts of yourself and giving up your interests and goals.
- Second guessing your choices and not making the best decisions for yourself.

- Engaging in negative self-talk.
- Addictive behaviors (sex, food, drugs)

None of these things are healthy for us. Whether you have experienced a couple of these things or more than a couple, we must learn to be our own advocate. We must know our limits and have the courage to speak up when we need to. Sometimes it can be scary to do things that are outside of our normal behavior but guess what? We were not created to function like robots. We need that balance; that time to unwind mentally from the day-to-day cycle of life and enjoy the things that we love. Make a commitment to make yourself a priority. Will you create the necessary balance that is needed in your life? Sometimes we have to say no to others, to say yes to ourselves.

Show up for YOU, even when no one else will.

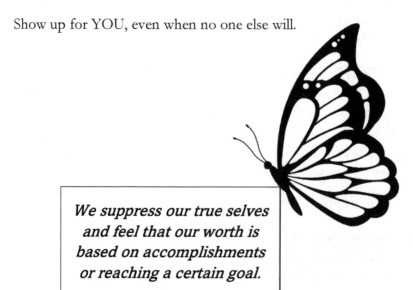

We suppress our true selves and feel that our worth is based on accomplishments or reaching a certain goal.

When you think about your life and the people in it, are there things that you could do differently in order to make yourself a priority? Many times, we fail to give ourselves what we really need for fear of being judged by others. We may think that other people will view us as selfish, lazy or uncompassionate. Do you want to know something? We tend to judge ourselves way more than other people do. That voice in our heads is typically our worst critic. For example, people who are A-type personalities like me, tend to be overly ambitious, outgoing, intense, values time management, are status conscious and not the best with patience. (I can admit that.) But I can definitely say that I have ignored my own needs on several occasions in the past because of how I did NOT want to be perceived by others. This has happened with personal and professional relationships. The value in understanding what self-abandonment looks like has allowed me to be more aware of situations where I am presented with the choice to either listen to my needs or ignore them due to self-judgment. At some point we have to realize that our needs are important and have value.

There are times when we can unknowingly ignore our needs. People who are caretakers for others or who are just naturally giving, can overlook their own needs. Or you could be someone who expects others to return the same love and appreciation to you that you so freely give. We have to focus on self-love and appreciation so that we don't fall into the trap of needing others for validation. While we do need to show compassion to others, it is as equally important to show compassion towards ourselves. What person knows you better than yourself? At the deepest part of your core, you have dreams, beautiful memories and special treasures that make you feel loved, happy, peaceful, and worthy. Don't be afraid to tap into those places or invest in those areas of your life. Regardless of whether you are a mother, daughter, sister, aunt, or grandmother, you cannot live your best life the way that God intended if you refuse to do what is necessary for yourself. You deserve His best.

Sometimes we have to say no to others, to say yes to ourselves.

SELF REFLECTIONS

No one knows us or what we need better than ourselves. We should not allow guilt or any other negative emotion to stop us from showing love to ourselves. Remember to re-fill your cup before pouring into others.

1. **Are there healthy boundaries in my life? If no, why not?**

_____
_____
_____
_____
_____

2. **What interests or talents have I put on the back burner?**

_____
_____
_____
_____
_____

3. **Do I have a hard time saying no to people?**

_____
_____
_____
_____
_____

4. What is at risk if I don't make some changes?

_____

_____

_____

_____

_____

Part II- The Cocoon

Abuse

"The Lord is close to the brokenhearted and saves those who are crushed in spirit."

-Psalm 34:18 (NIV)

There is a huge problem in the United States that many people have unfortunately been a victim of. It is almost impossible to turn on the news or read an online article without seeing numerous cases regarding it. There are many forms, and while they may differ, the effects are remarkably similar; feelings of devastation, behavioral, emotional, or physical changes, and a multitude of other issues for those who have been violated. The problem that I am talking about is abuse. Abuse is defined as intentionally causing harm or injury to another person. It may be physical, emotional/mental, or sexual and it is illegal in the United States. It is estimated that almost 9 million cases of domestic partner abuse occur each year. Regardless of the type of abuse that occurs, it is never acceptable and if you or someone else have been a victim you do not have to remain one.

Chapter Four

The Darkest Days

L et me begin by saying this: no one has the right to put their hands on you. There is nothing anyone can do that justifies this type of behavior. Genesis 1:27 says that God created us all in His own image. Our bodies were not created to be empty vessels and I know that He desires nothing but the best for us. Our bodies (temple), mind and spirit should honor Him and be treated with love because He took the time to carefully sculpt and breathe life into us. Physical abuse contradicts what God intended for His creations.

Physical abuse involves any action that causes harm to you at the hands of another person. It can include many things such as hitting, kicking, choking, pulling hair, burning or the use of a weapon. In addition, it can also include being physically restrained or threatened. Although anyone can be victimized, women and children are the ones more likely to be victims of physical abuse.

According to her Healthy Place article, Natasha Tracy says that women who are victims of physical abuse usually fall into one of the categories below:

- Controlling domestic relationships
- Elderly
- Physically or developmentally disabled
- Mentally ill
- Substance abusers
- Old cultural familial beliefs
- Households dealing with financial strain

Falling into one of these categories does not mean that you will automatically be a victim of physical abuse. It simply shows what the risk factors could be. At the same time, you can come from a seemingly perfect environment and still become a victim of physical abuse. If someone is prone to abusive behavior, he or she will victimize people regardless of race, age, religion, gender, or class. There have been numerous times where I have read or heard about someone being victimized and it shocked me. Not because it seemed impossible, but because I just never expected it. We never know what is going on behind closed doors. Just like the saying goes, "all that glitters is not gold." Don't believe everything that you see.

So, what is abuse about and what characteristics do abusers have? People who are physically abusive towards others want control. They need to feel powerful in order to hide the real issue which is typically insecurity. This insecurity may stem from failures in their personal or professional life which then shows up in a relationship. I knew a couple that fit this exact scenario. The husband had a decent job and was able to provide for his family which allowed the wife to pursue some of her personal goals. However, something happened with his job, and he blamed her for it. He felt that if he had been able to pursue his dreams before he got married and had children, then he would have been in a better place financially. Now we know that his disappointment was not her fault. His inability to acknowledge the truth caused him to lash out at the person who was probably the closest to him. The verbal abuse she had endured for years became physical. Sadly, this does tend to happen within many relationships. Although alcohol and drugs are not the main cause of abuse, they can be involved.

While there is no foolproof way to determine who is capable of physical abuse, there are common characteristics that we should look out for. These include jealousy, aggressiveness, trust issues, clinginess, animal cruelty, and possessiveness. According to a study completed by Florida Atlantic University, men who tend to fall into abusive patterns utilize certain tactics referred to as mate retention behaviors, to keep tabs on their victims.

Data was collected from over 1,000 men who shared the tactics they used to control their significant other as well as from over 500 women who shared their experiences with their partners. In the minds of these men, they needed to be reassured that their partner wasn't cheating or attempting to leave the relationship. As a result, they took drastic measures such as:

- Dropping by their partner's house unannounced
- Calling them to see if they are where they claimed to be
- Making personal threats toward their partner
- Occupying all of their partner's time
- Using manipulation to control

Remember, abusive behavior is usually hidden in the beginning and gradually emerges over time. Keep an eye out for these signs and seek help if you are noticing them in your relationship.

- Keeping you away from friends and family
- Embarrassing you in public
- Threatening to kill themselves
- Telling you that you aren't allowed to work
- Pressuring you to use drugs
- Harming your pets or property
- Doing anything that makes you feel uncomfortable

- Blaming you for everything that goes wrong
- Following you

> **People who are physically abusive towards others want control.**

Now I am sure you can think of people that you know or have encountered with some of these traits. Every abuser won't have the same characteristics, but these are red flags to look out for. There will forever be a moment in my life where I wish I could have foreseen the traumatic event that would take place one night. I moved to South Florida with my two children about 13 years ago for a new career. I was excited and nervous at the same time because I knew no one there. I had made the decision to step out on faith. Since God blessed me with this opportunity, I knew He would be with me every step of the way. I quickly learned my new role, met some nice people, and found a church that I liked. My children were adjusting to their new lives as well.

After about a year, things were still going great. My children had developed friendships and I had a close circle of people that I could depend on. Being a Florida girl, I enjoyed being down south. I could head to South Beach, any one of the Keys, or the local nurseries and wineries. The culture was vastly different but in a good way. I immersed myself into the culture and even took up Spanish classes. I decided to give dating a try since that had not been my focus. One guy captured my attention. He seemingly had a lot of the qualities that were important to me. We went out to dinner, watched movies, went dancing, had great intellectual conversations, and enjoyed each other when we were in each other's presence. He knew that I was not looking to be physically involved and he said that it was not an issue for him.

It was the summertime, and my children were spending time with family back home. He told me that he was taking me to dinner. I was excited because there were so many restaurants that I hadn't been to. We enjoyed dinner and had a fantastic time. He brought me back home and made sure that I was inside safely. Before he left, he went to use the restroom and when he came out, he seemed different. It was not a look or a vibe that I was used to. You know how our gut tells us that something just ain't right? Before I realized it, I was punched in the face and immediately tasted blood. My tooth had been knocked out. I was terrified and confused. Why was he doing this to me? Before I could run or try to defend myself, he pulled a gun on me.

He made me turn the tv on and instructed me to raise the volume. He grabbed my trembling body and pushed my face down onto the floor. As he ripped my clothes off, I pleaded with him to stop. With tears in my eyes, I told him he didn't have to do this. He only said two words to me, and they were "shut up". As he proceeded to rape me, I lay frozen; my cries drowned out by the tv. The weight of him on me and the sweat mixed with the cologne I once loved, would leave a tragic memory that I would never forget. Though I could no longer see the gun, I knew he still had it. Was he going to kill me? I could only think of my babies and how much I loved them.

When he was done, he warned me that he would kill me and my children if I told anyone. I believed him. After he left, I stayed on the floor for what felt like an eternity. My world as I once known it had just come crashing down on me. There were so many painful emotions existing within me, and I felt completely empty. I was devastated. I was broken. I was angry with myself for allowing someone to get close to me. I wondered what I had done to deserve this. I vowed to never trust anyone again. But the need to protect my children kicked in and I went into survival mode. I had to change my focus from the disgust that I felt about myself to doing what was best for my family. I searched until I found us a new place in another city. I honestly do not know how I hid my pain for so long from them, my family members, or coworkers. The tooth that I lost was not completely visible when I smiled so that part was easy to hide until I could get to a dentist. Thankfully, I never saw that guy again, but I walked on eggshells for a long time never knowing if I would. The journey to healing was extremely rough but through prayer, counseling, and re-learning to love myself, I overcame. I found myself again. Little did I know that my traumatic experience would fuel a passion for helping women to overcome their own personal traumas.

The Rape Crisis Center lists some of the statistics on sexual assault:

- A person is assaulted every 98 seconds.
- 1 out of every 6 women has been a victim in her lifetime.
- About 55% of assaults occur near the victim's home; followed by public places or a relative's home.
- Approximately 48% of victims are sleeping, traveling, or running errands.
- Victims are often between the ages of 18-34, followed by the age range of 35-64.
- Child victims typically range between 12-17.
- About 15% of victims know their attacker.

> *Little did I know that my traumatic experience would fuel a passion for helping women to overcome their own personal traumas.*

I would not want anyone to go through what I did. Regardless of your traumatic experience or someone that is close to you, there are steps that you can take to try in order to protect yourself and the ones that you love:

- Create an emergency plan.
- Have somewhere that you can go for safety.
- Make extra keys and put them in places that only you would know of.
- Keep important papers together and readily accessible.
- Open a separate bank account in your name only.

Domestic abuse usually happens in phases. There is the phase where stress and tension build up from the daily cycle of work, kids, and other issues. Eventually that tension leads to episodes of verbal and physical abuse. The abuser may also try to isolate you from your friends and family or control you in other ways. Whenever this episode is over which can last from a few hours to a few weeks, the abuser enters the reconciliation or honeymoon phase. There are numerous apologies, gifts, or other efforts to make the victim think the abuse will never happen again. Unfortunately, the cycle only repeats itself.

The effects of physical abuse can vary from person to person. However, there are common traits such as depression, post- traumatic stress disorder, anxiety, hopelessness, emotional eating, drug or alcohol abuse, trust issues and suicidal thoughts. I dealt with several of these. I felt dead on the inside and the emotional connection to food became soothing to me. Think about how good you feel when you have your favorite sweet treat. In that moment, you are basking in the flavors that are swirling around on the inside of your mouth. If you're anything like me, you might hum or dance a little bit because it's so good! Just like a drug, that "high" only lasts for so long until you crash from the sugar. The reality of your life returns until you can do something to feel good again.

If you are involved in an abusive situation, the primary goal is your safety. Please do not remain in a situation that could end up taking your life or the life of someone you care about. One of my favorite bible verses is Psalm 34:4-5. "I sought the Lord, and He answered me. He delivered me from all of my fears. Those who look to Him are radiant; their faces are never covered with shame." You are stronger than you think. What I went through almost destroyed me, but I refused to allow it and you don't have to allow your pain to destroy you either.

Unfortunately, the cycle only repeats itself.

SELF REFLECTIONS

In order to heal from abuse, we must assess it from many angles. It is not the easiest thing to do but necessary for recovery and growth.

1. **Are my views of relationships healthy?**

_____

_____

_____

_____

_____

2. **What has stopped me from making changes for a better life?**

_____

_____

_____

_____

_____

3. **Am I willing to face my fears and confront my shame?**

_____

_____

_____

_____

_____

4. **Will I do the work healing requires and not give up on myself?**

_____

_____

_____

_____

_____

Chapter Five

A Cracked Egg

"Sticks and stones may break my bones, but words will never hurt me." Do you remember this childhood rhyme? It was quite common as I was growing up. It takes me back to the good ole days of playing Hopscotch, Duck Duck Goose, and picking up Jackstones. My grandmother didn't play about being inside when that streetlight came on! You'd better tell your friends that you would see them tomorrow. As nostalgic as that rhyme is, it couldn't be further from the truth. Words CAN hurt.

While the signs of physical abuse are more obvious, emotional, and mental abuse are typically harder to notice. Emotional abuse involves humiliation, isolation, blame, criticism, patterns of abusive language, creating fear and guilt. The aim is to control the victim and destroy his or her self-esteem. This type of abuse can occur in various types of relationships: professional, familial, romantic, and close friendships. You may have experienced one or more of these things over the course of your life, but it is the constant pattern of demeaning behavior that signifies the abuse. The abuser continually tries to make you feel inadequate and inferior.

The abuser seeks to dominate their victims because they fear being controlled themselves. They often feel as though they have the right to do this because they are owed something. Have you ever known anyone who came across as entitled and self-centered? I can recall a few people. Let us look at some of the characteristics of emotional abusers.

- Exhibit extreme jealousy and/or paranoia
- Have low self-esteem
- Unrealistic demands
- May be an alcoholic
- Critical of everything
- Gaslights the victim into believing they are at fault
- Refusing to give personal space
- Shows favoritism between siblings
- Utilizes name calling

A lot of these characteristics aren't obvious to people outside of the relationship. You could see the same person every day at work or in social environments and never know that they are an abuser. You know how people are, they put on their best faces. When we want to make a positive impression on others, we do and say the right things. I mean I have done that when interviewing for a job for example. But with abuse, it is more of turning the behavior on and off when needed in an attempt to hide it. (Dr. Jekyll and Mr. Hyde anyone?) He or she never wants to come across as the bad person. As a matter of fact, the victim is usually blamed for causing the abuse. There may be statements made such as, "You made me do it." Or "If only you had done what I told you to do."

There have been numerous occasions where I have encountered people who never take responsibility for their actions. There is always an excuse for why it wasn't his or her fault. When we don't accept our part in a situation, it shows immaturity, and it is also an attempt to protect our ego. Even though deep down inside the person knows that they are not being truthful. Remember, their image is important regardless of how the other person feels.

Mental and emotional abuse are linked to personality disorders. There are three main types: Antisocial, Narcissistic, and borderline personality disorder. People with these disorders develop toxic patterns of behavior over the course of their lives. According to Dr. Dharius Daniels, when pain is mismanaged, it becomes a part of our personality.

Antisocial personality:

Those who suffer with this disorder are often involved in criminal activity. They are often deceptively charming and manipulative and only interested in doing things for their personal gain. (Think Jeffrey Dahmer and Ted Bundy.) Antisocial personalities have a cynical attitude, are cocky and very impulsive. There is also the ability to hurt others without showing any remorse. This disorder is believed to stem from child abuse or from having parents with the same personality disorder.

Narcissistic personality:

People with this personality disorder have an extremely high sense of self-importance, arrogance, and a superiority complex. It is their thought pattern that they are entitled to power and fame, and they may lie about credentials and achievements to try to impress others. Because their emotions change quickly, it is hard for people to maintain relationships with narcissists. This disorder is also grounded in emotional abuse from childhood. Unfortunately, I am very familiar with narcissistic behavior, and I also attended school with someone who displayed these traits. Do you know what her childhood was like? Her parents were overbearing, overly critical of everything she did and emotionally abusive. I'm sure that this led to her personal views of herself and how she treated others, including me. I had to decide to end that friendship with her in order to keep my sanity. Ain't nobody got time for that! Is there anyone in your life past or present that falls into this category?

Borderline personality:

Those with borderline personality disorder have issues with how they see themselves and other people. They have extreme highs and lows, fear of rejection, and unstable emotions. It is sometimes hard for them to focus on reality, and they may try to harm themselves by engaging in drugs, promiscuous sex, or suicidal thoughts. Just like the narcissistic and antisocial personalities, borderline personalities are connected to emotional trauma and dysfunction.

> ***The abuser seeks to dominate their victims because they fear being controlled themselves.***

The effects of emotional and mental abuse run deep and tend to be long lasting. Those who have been victims may experience feelings of fear, confusion, shame, or hopelessness. Over the course of time adults can develop issues such as anxiety, chronic illnesses or become socially withdrawn. Children may develop eating disorders, mental health disorders or become clingy.

When I think about mental and emotional abuse, it really saddens me. I think about the number of people who have had to experience this type of abuse. It also takes me back to various points in my life where I felt invisible. As the oldest child, I felt like I had a lot of responsibility. I had weekly chores that included washing and hanging clothes on the line for the entire family (when the dryer wasn't working). Also, cleaning, dusting, vacuuming, and babysitting the youngest two siblings. As I have said before, I believe in children having chores, but I often felt that those things overshadowed the affection and emotional attention that I craved from my parents. I know they loved me, but those things weren't always expressed. When my father was home, he was often playful, enjoyed playing music or watching sports. He would also share helpful words of wisdom from time to time, but I had both a desire and need to be seen, heard and soothed. I felt as if my individuality was lost. This is important because the older a child gets, he or she needs to be able to create a sense of self.

As I got older, I gravitated towards relationships that had a level of toxicity to them. Constant arguing, gaslighting, and controlling behaviors seemed normal. I found myself accepting things that I now know are unacceptable. After all, life always seemed to present challenges in one area or another. But just like before, I would deal with them in my own way. That typically meant showing everyone the "everything is fine" face while I was secretly hurting on the inside. Have you ever felt that way? It is hard trying to manage those feelings, especially by ourselves. Prayer is always first in my life but sometimes we need to speak to someone to express those feelings and there is nothing wrong with that. The negative stigma that surrounds therapy can easily deter people from seeking help. There are a number of reasons why people get counseling. Yes, some are due to mental illness, but many people need someone to talk to regarding the emotional issues that life can bring about. Just as we visit doctors for our other health concerns, we should be able to seek help from a therapist without feeling ashamed. The pressure of caring what other people think of us should not outweigh the importance of taking steps toward self-improvement.

Keep in mind that if you do connect with a therapist, the process is not something that you should expect to complete within a few days. The issues that influenced your decision to seek counseling did not happen overnight, so it will take time to reflect and do the necessary work towards healing. What works for one person may not work for the next, and it may take a few tries to find the right therapist for you but don't give up! Please understand that you are not alone in your struggles. There are many people who seek professional counseling but are hesitant to share that information with others. This is due to all of the misconceptions about those who attend therapy sessions. Taking the step to seek counseling does not mean that you are weak, alone, crazy, holding on to the past, or on meds. As a matter of fact, taking that step shows a great deal of bravery. You are doing what so many chose not to do. It also does not mean that you are without a strong support system. Our friends, while being pretty good listeners are not therapists. Everyone has a specific role in our lives. The role of the therapist is not to make us forget our past, but to help us breakdown some of the unresolved areas of our lives, and work through any lingering issues. I know that this is usually seen as a highly personal matter for many but showing our strength in the ability to take a stand for a better quality of life could inspire others to do the same.

Our emotional well-being matters just as much as the physical. In the times that we are living in and currently being amid a global pandemic, many people have sought counseling. If you feel that it is right for you and you are ready, maybe you should try it. You can also write, join a support group, or express yourself through various forms of creativity. Sometimes we are hurting but we are completely unaware of it.

If you do decide to give counseling a shot, know that choosing a therapist is not something that should be done hastily. You should research the type of therapist that you are seeking. Look at their credentials, look at their pictures, determine if you prefer a woman or a man. Even deciding on the age range that you might prefer is of importance. Maybe you would feel more comfortable with an older woman or man who has had more life experiences. Or you may want someone who has a particular background. The choice is all yours because you want to select someone that will be the right fit for you.

There is a difference between a licensed mental health therapist and a life coach. Therapists must pass licensure requirements and uphold certain standards. Life coaches on the other hand, are not required to have a degree.

Before you have your first visit, there are some things that you may want to do:

- Find out if the therapist offers consultations. This will allow you to ask questions about their counseling style or what to expect.
- Make a list of what you want to accomplish in your sessions.
- Determine what you hope to gain from the therapy.
- Remember that what you discuss is confidential.
- Be proud of yourself for taking the first step.
- Practice mediation and/or breathing exercises to lower your anxiety
- Allow yourself time to open up.
- You are not "locked in" just because you had one session. Feel free to change therapists if you don't feel he or she is the best fit for your needs.

> **The pressure of caring what other people think of us should not outweigh the importance of taking steps toward self-improvement.**

One day, I was listening to the radio and the DJ was speaking to a mental health therapist by the name of Dr. Bev. They were discussing various topics on families and relationships. The therapist seemed to be very knowledgeable, down to earth and she gave some great tips that spoke to me. She started to make regular appearances on the show, and I looked forward to the dialogue between her and the other listeners who would call in. Deep down inside, I knew that I had some unresolved issues that I needed to dissect. With all of the courage inside of me, I took a leap and called her office to set up an appointment. So many things were going through my mind: was I ready to be vulnerable with her? Honest with myself? I was willing to try it out. We had several sessions and I realized that there was so much pain, resentment, and deep-rooted scars that I had not dealt with. I had been told of how my mother would go to get donuts and often carry me with her. Maybe this is why sweets often comforted me. Those sessions with Dr. Bev helped me in more ways than I can explain, but I walked away with so much strength and determination to get my power back. I am thankful for that experience, and I know that she is always a phone call away should I need her.

It is mind blowing to me when I reflect on moments in my life as an adult and recall things that were red flags or things that were ignored. Or look back at how I made decisions in certain situations. The list could go on and on. The key thing to remember is that we are not defined by the things that we went through, and we are not at the root cause. Either we make a choice to grow from those experiences or be ruined by them. I chose to grow. As tempting as it is to live in moments of regret, I realize that everything that I went through was a lesson or a test. As unfortunate as these experiences were, they did not destroy me. I realize that God was always in the driver's seat and many things that happened to me increased my faith in Him. I honestly believe that they all made me stronger, wiser, and more resilient. God has kept me here on this earth because my job is not done, and I am immensely grateful for His undying love.

SELF REFLECTIONS

Recovery is a process. Your timeline may not mirror someone else's, and it should not. You are resilient and an overcomer. Believe that healing is possible and begin to take the steps toward it one step at a time.

1. **When you think about the abuse that you experienced, do you blame yourself?**

_____
_____

2. **Do you have a support system?**

_____
_____

3. **Have you taken your power back? If not, what are you willing to do in order to regain it?**

_____
_____
_____
_____
_____

4. **When is the last time that you celebrated yourself?**

_____
_____

Chapter Six

Wolves Among Us

When I see children, many thoughts come to mind. I love the beauty in their eyes, their joyous laughter, and the pure innocence they possess without a care in the world. They are not concerned with the problems of adulthood. Children don't have to wake up and prepare breakfast, get ready for work, deal with the headaches of traffic or pay bills. And that is how it is supposed to be. They should be enjoying the things created for them: toys, bikes, games, sports and going to fun places.

Unfortunately, there is something despicable that threatens the innocence of our children. I am talking about sexual abuse which is also called molestation. Sexual abuse involves unwanted contact between a child and an adult. The abuser takes advantage of the child's inability to consent, or the child may even be fooled into doing something that is inappropriate. Most of the sexual abuse occurs between people who know each other. This is to the abuser's advantage especially if there is a level of trust already established. Abusers can be male or female, close family friends or sadly even relatives. Most cases of sexual abuse go unreported for several reasons. The victim may be afraid to tell someone or may think that no one will believe them. Or they may not understand that what is being done to them is wrong.

Here are some of the characteristics of child sexual abusers:

- Loneliness
- Sexual issues
- Poor social skills
- Difficulty maintaining adult relationships
- Low self-esteem

There are two types of sexual abuse. It can be by physical contact or non-physical contact. Physical contact is when direct contact is made by the abuser. It can include the following:

- Inappropriate touching of a child's body parts with or without clothing
- Using body parts or other objects to penetrate a child
- Forcing a child to perform sexual acts on another person

Non-physical contact is abuse that occurs without touch and can include the following:

- Showing pornography to a child
- Engaging them in sexual conversations online or via phone
- Taking pictures or video of a child in sexual positions
- Exposing genitals to a child

Depending on the abuser's mentality, there may be various methods used to introduce the abuse to the child. There may be gifts involved, playing of games, persuasion with the promise of receiving something if they cooperate or it may involve threats. Sickening, right? Sadly, we all know someone who has been sexually abused. Now whether that information has been shared with you is a different matter. According to the CDC, 1 in 4 girls and 1 in 13 boys are abused during childhood. That is just how common this type of abuse is. But why is it always kept a secret? Especially within families. Secrets destroy those relationships along with trust and often cause division between the people involved and sometimes it is unrepairable.

For the victim, he or she may experience self-doubt, feelings of confusion, anxiety, anger, or shame. Or there may be a combination of those feelings going on such as, who do I tell? Will that person confront my abuser? Will they protect me? Will I be taken from my home? Was this my fault? The child may feel like he or she has to choose sides. I am sure that a situation like that would be terrifying for a child. The reason I am so sure of that, is because I was that child.

Matthew 7:15 (NIV) says, "Watch out for false prophets. They come to you in sheep's clothing, but inwardly they are ferocious wolves." When I think about a wolf, I see an image of a sneaky, cunning, and dangerous predator. The abuse that I experienced started around the age of eight and lasted until I was around twelve. This person was family by marriage so I would see him off and on while visiting other family members. He was always smiling and was seemingly nice. At least in my eight-year-old eyes, so there was a level of trust there.

I don't remember how the touching started. Anytime he would come to visit, I would always sit on his lap. After all, he was always playful and nice. I remember wondering why this man was putting his hands in my secret place. I felt confused, nervous, and uneasy because I didn't understand what was happening. I was just beginning to learn about my body and the changes that were going on as a young girl and here was someone else invading and exploring it. As time went on, it became normal in a sense. I believed that this was just how things were supposed to go with him. How was I supposed to know that these activities were reserved for adults? No one had ever talked to me about abuse. I started to become more aware of my body. I had questions about what I was experiencing but I couldn't talk to anyone because I was afraid. Why didn't anyone else notice what was going on? So, I allowed those questions to just fade away.

I never told anyone until I became an adult. I was ashamed. I had a fear of what would happen to me and my family. On occasion I would see him if he came by to speak to family and I recall still feeling very uncomfortable. To see this despicable person smiling and talking as if he wasn't the lowest scum of the earth made me sick to my stomach. A family member once asked me why I acted cold towards him.

Thinking back on those years, I used to wonder what it was about me that made him choose me. I was quiet and self-conscious about my body image. Did he see me as the little vulnerable sheep? I often look back at pictures of myself from my younger years and I see so much sadness. Couldn't the people around me every day see this? I only wanted to be seen. Shame will tell us that we are not worth the attention; that we're only as important as what we can do. Shame doesn't belong to us. It is something that I should have never had to carry. Regardless of what my abuser's reasons were, I had to realize that the abuse and shame were not my fault. Abuse is never our fault.

Victims of child sexual abuse are affected in different ways. Many times, the feelings of shame turn into self-blame. The victim might be angry at themselves for not being strong enough to resist the abuse or may think they enticed the abuser in some way. This thought pattern can also lead to coping mechanisms such as eating disorders, depression, anxiety, or promiscuous behavior later in life. In relationships, victims may accept bad treatment from others because they don't believe they deserve better. My coping mechanisms were comfort eating, not letting people get close to me and burying my emotions. As a child, I never had a voice, so I created my own safety net.

My lack of control in that abusive situation molded me into an adult who needed to be in control as a parent, in relationships, and even in work environments. I need clearly defined agendas at work, and I am very task oriented. I would even say that I am a perfectionist in some areas. Could this stem from feeling as though I never did anything right? Maybe it's been my own way of providing a sense of security because I know that I can count on me. It is only within the last few years that I have learned that I don't always have to be so tough in an effort to protect my fragile shell. In what ways have you tried to cope with the trauma that you experienced? Have you discovered healthier ways to process it? It wasn't until I stopped seeing myself as a victim, that I began to choose better ways of coping. I learned that I didn't have to keep things inside anymore. Whether I spoke to someone about my feelings or journaled, I did my best to release that weight on my shoulders because I knew that it wasn't mine to carry.

Shame will tell us that we aren't worth the attention; that we're only as important as what we can do. Shame doesn't belong to us.

The thing that I constantly had to remind myself about the abuse, is that I was a child. A child that was not responsible for the actions of an adult. Abusers thrive on having power and control. If they can create an environment that makes the child believe that it is his or her fault, they are unlikely to tell anyone. That is manipulation at its core. No matter how long ago the abuse occurred in your life, you must understand that none of the guilt belongs to you. Accept that you WERE victimized so that guilt and shame can be released. There are times where I am reminded of what happened, and it's okay. However, I try not to remain in that space because I have come too far. As strong women, we already have enough to carry in this world and we certainly don't need to carry anything that doesn't belong to us.

At the same time, we each have a different path to recovery from abuse and it takes time. For some, the process may be lifelong depending on the level of trauma one experienced. Many times, we may feel that we have put the trauma behind us and vowed to never look back, only to be triggered by something that puts us right back in the place we never wanted to return. According to Merriam-Webster, a trigger is something that causes an intense and negative reaction in a person. You may be wondering if there is anything that you can do to prepare for triggers. Unfortunately, the answer is no. We have no way of knowing when or how we will be triggered. Anything can cause a reaction, whether that is a certain sound, smell, or even being in a particular place. We've all been there.

When we are reminded of a painful time in our lives, our bodies release automatic responses in an effort to protect us from harm. This is similar to how our immune systems go into a fight or flight mode when we are exposed to viruses or bacteria. While this is normal, we cannot allow triggers to affect us to the point where we are unable to function as we typically do. If we can learn to respond vs. reacting to the triggers, it will help us recover quicker. For example, say that you are triggered by a song that comes on the radio. Your involuntary response to the song makes you feel sadness or anxiety in that moment. Those feelings are valid because they may represent a very dark time in your life.

However, instead of allowing those feelings to send you overboard, you are able to use some techniques that you may have learned. The healing process is similar to a skin cut in that it takes time for a scab to develop and sometimes that scab gets picked at during the healing process. If we are able to give it special care, that will aid in the healing process.

Triggers typically fall into nine categories:

- Feeling taken advantage of or used.
- Feeling vulnerable in a situation that invokes a feeling of being exposed.
- Feeling self-conscious amongst a group of people.
- When our boundaries are threatened.
- Feeling uncomfortable while witnessing a violent situation.
- Being fearful of imminent danger.
- Issues in relationships.
- Being discounted or ignored.
- Being controlled by others.

It is highly possible that you have or will experience one or more of these situations in your lifetime. When we deal with people in our personal lives, at work or in other various environments, we are exposed to many different stimuli. Having access to helpful tools when we are experiencing an emotional reaction is crucial to our emotional health. In addition, it may be beneficial to have a therapist who is familiar with the effects of childhood trauma so they can help you reach the deep-rooted issues that we are sometimes afraid to re-visit.

While the therapist is trained in helping those who are struggling with childhood trauma, we are the ones who must do the work. The therapist is there to support us along the way. Also, keep in mind that you may have to try more than one therapist or different types of therapy before you find one that you are comfortable with. Never feel forced to stick with it if it does not work. There are a vast amount of support groups and organizations out there. Healing is about you, no one else.

The following tips may also aid in your healing journey.

- Trust that you are safe now. You don't have to hide anymore.
- Validate and acknowledge your feelings about the abuse.
- Allow yourself to have emotions and do not suppress them.
- Grieve what was taken from you in childhood. Crying is therapeutic and helps to release built up trauma.
- Move forward. You can remember what happened to you, but don't linger there. Your future is calling you.
- Don't compare your healing process to anyone else's.
- Realize that you will have good days and bad days.
- Learn a new craft, practice daily meditation, or exercise.

No matter where you are in your healing process, realize that you deserve to live your life without being held captive by the dark places of your past. Shame, unworthiness, and doubt live there. The ability to see the light at the end of the tunnel starts with us being ready to start the healing process. It is something liberating about speaking our truth. Break the silence. Your path to freedom is on the other side.

We each have a different path to recovering from abuse and it does take time.

SELF REFLECTIONS

We are not what happens to us. It is important to look back and reflect on our past in order to move forward in the present towards healing.

1. Have you allowed your pain to control how you interact with others?

    _____
    _____
    _____

2. What lies have you told yourself and believed? Write them down. Next, work on discovering truths in place of those lies.

    _____
    _____
    _____
    _____
    _____

3. Has the abuse that you experienced fueled a new passion in your life?

    _____
    _____
    _____
    _____
    _____

4. You are still here. You survived. Make a list of your strengths and how you will continue to thrive throughout your journey to healing.

_____

_____

_____

_____

_____

_____

_____

_____

_____

_____

_____

_____

_____

Part III- Emerging

Transformation

"Being confident of this very thing, that He who has begun a good work in you will complete it until the day of Jesus Christ."

-Philippians 1:6 (NKJV)

The process of transformation can be frightening, intimidating, and filled with uncertainty. Or it can be filled with beauty, hope and anticipation. Regardless of where we are in life, change is inevitable. As we grow through life many times our habits, thoughts, feelings, personal preferences, and value systems change. For many people, this process takes time, but we can utilize that time to our advantage. When we look back on all the pain we endured or may be enduring, I believe we can also uncover some important things about ourselves. (They have always been there.) I learned that I am strong, determined, resilient and triumphant! However, one of the most important things that I learned was how to love myself again. I slowly began to see myself through a new set of lenses which made it easier to actively engage in activities that built me up instead of tearing me down. That self-love I possessed, led me to put it into action by practicing something called self-care.

Chapter Seven

Love on yourself

What is self-care? Self-care is involving ourselves in things that cater to our emotional, mental, and physical health. It is how we stay mindful of our own needs. In a crazy world that says we can't slow down; we have to create balance to reduce stress and overall well-being. We are moms, wives, sisters, aunties, grandmothers, and many other things to others which demands a lot of our time and energy. I love the saying, "You can't pour from an empty cup." In other words, if you do not take time to refuel yourself physically, mentally, and spiritually, your gas tank is going to run out. That sounds easy, right?

The problem is that a lot of times we don't believe we are deserving of the attention. We have responsibilities which are usually placed in a higher category of importance. So, it is quite easy to forget that we have essential needs as well. One of the hardest things to do is to love ourselves unconditionally, with all of our shortcomings and flaws. Everything that is advertised on tv, and social media focuses on imperfections. Not in a positive light that celebrates our unique differences, but in a way that says we have to fix what is broken. This is why we cannot rely on external sources to reinforce self-love and the need for self-care. Until we can be completely real with ourselves about who we are and what our needs are, we will not see the value in self-care.

If you were to ask most people if they love themselves, the answer would be yes. But love is an action word and most of the time those actions do not line up with our words. The act of loving ourselves go beyond making sure we look cute in that certain outfit, having the perfect lipstick, or keeping our hair and nails done. Surely all of those things are nice and enjoyable, but there is so much more that is needed. It is not about the amount of money we spend on ourselves. Sometimes it is as simple as going for a walk and embracing the sound of the birds, or the warmth of the sun on a beautiful day. Other times, it may be going for a bike ride, visiting a coffee shop (coffee lover here) or going for a drive in your car. Self-love involves intentionality. It is making a conscious effort every single day to do what is best for our overall well-being.

This is why it's important to know what our needs are. When you think of relationships that you have been involved in or considered being in, was there a mental list of what qualities you were seeking? More than likely, you had a list of deal breakers, things that you absolutely would not stand for. Now let me ask you a question: do you have those same standards or expectations about yourself? Probably not. The most important relationship on Earth is the one that we have with ourselves. This is where it all starts. Learning to show love and appreciation for that person you see in the mirror can be an uphill battle, but it is possible. Instead of treating ourselves like someone who deserves kindness, attentiveness, compassion, respect, and encouragement, we tend to do the opposite.

We can end up being our own worst critic because instead of believing that we can finish the degree, land the dream job, start the business, or step out on faith, we allow self-pity, self-hatred, and feelings of unworthiness to take over. If we believe those negative thoughts, then our life will eventually reflect that. What if you had a friend who was going through a tough time in their life, and they needed someone to talk to? Would you be there for them? Being there could consist of many things. But I would imagine that it might involve listening, motivating, reassuring, or doing something to take their mind off of what is bothering them. Although this is what a friend would do for another person, it is also some of the very same things that we should do for ourselves. Self-care involves listening to our needs and believing that we can go after those needs without feeling selfish or guilty.

As a young woman, I had never heard of self- care. I only knew that I enjoyed getting my hair done, going shopping, reading, journaling, and listening to music. All of those things made me feel good. Little did I know that they were important for many reasons. Those things unknowingly gave me relief from everyday life. They were a way for me to get a personal reset.

Self-love involves intentionality. It is making a conscious effort every single day to do what is best for our overall well-being.

Although I enjoyed having those moments to myself, I always felt a sense of guilt. After all, I was a single mother who worked full time and at one point went back to get another college degree. I often wondered, what do my kids think of me? Sure, I had the support of my family, but I was momma. No one could care for them like I could. I had to be there for all of the events, field trips, and help with homework. When it was time for bed, I needed to be the one to tuck them in. You know, all of the things we do as parents and caregivers. It's just hard to balance it all sometimes. Thinking back to my childhood and being the oldest child, I was used to juggling a lot of things and I often created a daily schedule to keep things in line. That mindset carried over into my adulthood as well. So, as a parent it was easy to lose sight of the things that I needed. However, the older the kids got, it was a little easier to do more for myself because teens/young adults develop their own interests. They spend more time with friends than with us as they set out to make their own mark in the world. But they still need us. No matter how old they get, they still need our love, attention, and support.

Once I realized I wasn't failing my kids by taking time to recharge, it all seemed to click. If I was too tired, sick, or incapable of being there for them, how was that beneficial for any of us? I realized that I could not ride around on fumes, almost empty without it having negative consequences. When we are able to refuel, we can then be the best version of ourselves for the people in our lives.

It isn't just one thing to being able to take care of ourselves though. We have to believe we deserve that special care. This is where self-esteem comes into play. While self-care encompasses how we take care of ourselves, self-esteem stems from our overall view of our self-worth which then affects our overall wellness. I believe if we see ourselves in a positive light, then we are more likely to do things that are good for us.

> **Until we can be completely real with ourselves about who we are and what our needs are, we will not see the value in self-care.**

Friends and family can have an effect on whether your self-respect, self-image and self-confidence grows or diminishes. Whether you are given positive or negative feedback, teased or criticized, it will affect your self-esteem. Low self-esteem often arises as self-doubt, sensitivity to criticism, insecurity, limited social skills and depression. On the other hand, high self-esteem is often seen in healthy relationships, confidence in making decisions, the ability to openly communicate and feeling whole.

If you are like me, you didn't grow up with high self-esteem. Mine was actually pretty low which contributed to my loner lifestyle for many years. I had to work on it over a long period of time, especially after surviving many of the tragedies that I endured. Through prayer, meditation, counseling, journaling, and speaking daily affirmations to myself, I began to see myself as God sees me. Now I can't say that my self-esteem is at 100% all of the time either, but I have definitely experienced amazing growth in that area. Each one of us has different stories and journeys that we have been on and what works for one may not work for another. The key is to start somewhere on the path to loving ourselves.

It can be difficult to start, and I get that. In addition to the negative external influences, there are internal ones also. Many of us are consumed with what is going on in our heads. Before we can start working towards a thing, we have already counted all of the reasons why we can't or shouldn't do it. Have you ever thought any these things about yourself?

- I'm not smart enough.
- I don't have what it takes.
- I'm too old.
- I've made too many mistakes.
- I need to look a certain way.
- I can't do this because of what people will say.
- It's going to be hard.
- If my life was like this person's, it would be better.
- I can make time for myself later.
- What I have to share isn't really important.

Out of all of those statements, only one may be true. It's going to be hard. But just because something is hard, doesn't mean that it is impossible. The rest of those statements are negative self- talk and do not promote healthy self-esteem or wellness. Anytime we are doing something outside of our comfort zone or something we aren't used to doing, it won't come easily. But we have to see ourselves doing those things while believing that we are not only capable but deserving of the best things that life has to offer. You are one of the most important projects you will ever work on. So, make sure you give yourself some TLC. Self-care is not selfish. It is necessary. Even Jesus took time to withdraw from the people who were in need, to be alone and pray. It's not that He wasn't concerned with them, but He knew what He needed to do in order to regroup. (My introverts can relate.) When a person is acting in a selfish manner, they are only concerned with themselves regardless of the negative way it impacts others. Self-care allows us to focus on replenishing ourselves without taking from others. It gives us time to reflect, explore life, and maybe discover something new about ourselves. It is not only good for our bodies, but our minds as well. We are worthy of love, appreciation, validation and so much more! Here are some ways that we can practice self-care and also contribute to healthy esteem.

- Don't be afraid to say no to others. You don't have to agree to every request.
- Visit a spa. Schedule a massage or facial.
- Unplug from social media. There is a lot of negativity and who needs that?
- Exercise. You'll be amazed what it does for your mind and body.
- Journal your thoughts.
- Get enough sleep. You should be as refreshed as possible.
- Stop and appreciate all of the good in your life.
- Meditate and pray.
- Eat a nice piece of chocolate or have a glass of wine.
- Make a list of some of your best qualities.
- Enjoy a good movie or book.
- Hang out with a friend.

Of course, these are just suggestions. There are numerous ways to practice self-care and no method is better than the other. Remember, it takes intentional effort on our part. If we don't make time for self-care, then it will not happen. Showing ourselves love doesn't always require a three-day weekend, although I'm always down for an extended weekend! But we can engage in some self-care activities throughout the day. Ten to fifteen minutes here and there count as well. We schedule hair appointments, doctor's appointments, meetings, car maintenance appointments, even automatic bill pay so why not schedule time for ourselves? Regardless of what way you choose to practice self-care, just make sure it works for you. Our needs will change from time to time and that's okay. It may help to take a moment to access how you are feeling and what area is lacking attention in your life. After that, you can decide what form of self-care you need. Just take it one step at a time and remember you are worth it.

You are one of the most important projects that you will ever work on.

SELF REFLECTIONS

Self-care has to be a priority. Whether it's something that you do when waking, throughout the day or before bed, put time on your calendar for yourself. Ask yourself these questions.

1. **Who or what inspires me?**

_____

_____

_____

_____

2. **Will I make a choice not to betray myself while trying to please others?**

_____

_____

3. **Are there any areas of my life that I can remove negativity?**

_____

_____

_____

_____

4. **When do I feel that I'm at my best?**

_____

_____

_____

Chapter Eight

Health Matters

Health is defined as having total physical, mental, and social well-being as well as being free from disease. While I do agree that those are all major components to health, I do not totally agree with that definition. I believe that they all work together to contribute to a better standard of living, but just because one area of our health is better than the other it doesn't equate to unhealthiness. We all have different levels of physical, mental, and social health, right? In addition, how many people do you know that are not dealing with some type of health issue? Not too many, I'm sure. The key is how we manage and strive towards improving our health.

So, if having a better standard of living is supported by a healthy lifestyle, what does that really look like? Does that mean the same thing for someone in their 20's compared to a person who is in their 70's? What about someone who was born with a chronic illness compared to someone who is diagnosed years later? I believe there would be a completely different plan of care. An elderly person may not be able to fight the illness on the same level as the younger person. In order to really understand how important every area of our health is, it is important to discuss them individually first.

If you look at the world that we live in, strategies for managing our health are everywhere. We see commercials advertising the best solutions for our ailments, various pamphlets in doctor's offices, and pharmacies showcasing a variety of medications to take the pain away even if only temporarily. This is how many of us manage our physical health. We can do things that contribute to our physical health in order to limit our need for medication such as exercising, making good choices when it comes to food, and getting enough sleep. The benefits of having good physical health are many, but they include improving blood flow to our hearts, maintaining, or improving muscle strength, endurance, and flexibility. And it works wonders for stress! I have found that it also gives me more energy. Have you ever felt like not working out but after you did you felt amazing? Yes, I love that feeling while knowing that I did something good for my body as well. I am not a morning person and will probably never be, but I prefer to get my workouts done first thing in the morning. That way, I can start my workday feeling good and be ready for that first cup of coffee. Sometimes our days can get busy and unexpected things may pop up, so that planned evening workout doesn't always happen. Now I will tell you that there are those days where my alarm goes off and my pillow feels too good to abandon. But when it comes to your workout, it doesn't have to be strenuous. Aim for at least 25-30 minutes and do something that gets that heart rate going. You can take a walk, go for a bike ride, join a yoga class, or even do jump rope. There are so many ways to be active. Our ticker needs love y'all. We have to care for it and provide what it needs so that it can do its job.

I have always had pretty good health. From the time I was a young girl, until my early twenties I'd never been in the hospital. But when I was pregnant with my daughter during my fifth month, I began experiencing extreme stomach pains. The pain was unlike anything I had ever felt. It hurt regardless of whether I stood, sat, or laid down. I went to the emergency room where I was initially given meds for constipation and gas and sent home. One night, the pain was so intense that 911 was called out to my home. However, the medical personnel did not take me to the hospital because my vitals were normal. My grandmother was with me and because she did not drive, we decided to wait until the morning to go to the hospital. Other family members came and once we arrived at the E.R., we were told that I would need exploratory surgery because nothing showed on the sonogram. This news terrified me. Immediately I thought of my baby girl. Would she be okay? Would I be ok? By the grace of God, we both were. It was discovered that I had a blocked colon which was on the verge of rupturing. It was caught just in time! I know for a fact that God had a plan for my life and that my time was not finished yet. His covering was truly upon me.

My recovery was hard and also life changing since I had to temporarily live with a colostomy bag until after my daughter was born. I struggled with the questions like, why did this happen to me? Could I have prevented this? The answer was no. It was just a rare thing that happened. I also had to learn to embrace a new body. There were changes post-surgery that didn't exist before the procedure. Having to deal with the pain and anxiety of not knowing what was wrong with me prior to surgery and then awakening to a new me took its toll. Thankfully, I had a huge amount of love and support and the comfort of knowing that I was not alone. My daughter was born on her original due date, and it was a normal vaginal birth with no health issues. You cannot tell me that God doesn't work miracles!

What happened to me could have happened to anyone. The doctors said that there were only about 70 known cases of this happening to pregnant women. I didn't realize it at the time, but that situation would become a part of my testimony for how God was the head physician in the operating room on that day. The scars that remain are a part of me. They are an addition to my uniqueness, my strength, and my ability to persevere. To deny or be ashamed of them would take away from the beautiful gift of life that my daughter and I have. My scars are proof that I made it through the battle and are evidence of God's work. What started out as pain turned to praise! I am so thankful for His grace.

About fourteen years later, I started to experience stiff joints, migraines, and constant fatigue. After a series of tests, I was diagnosed with Lupus. I knew nothing about this autoimmune illness. No one in my family had it so I had to do research in order to learn about it. Lupus is a disease where the immune system attacks its own tissues and organs. Normally our immune system only attacks foreign bacteria and viruses but in Lupus, the immune system attacks the good as well. Every case is different along with the severity, but symptoms include chest pain, digestive issues, memory loss, extreme fatigue, hair loss, joint pain, skin lesions, migraines, dry mouth, nerve, organ damage and much more. Has Lupus affected my physical health? Yes. I have experienced many of those symptoms but thankfully nothing that has given me an overnight hospital stay. These symptoms are called flares.

A flare can be triggered by various factors such as stress, the sun, certain medications, an illness, injury, or even life changes. But I have learned how to manage it in the best way that works for me. I have been in this fight for several years and along with staying active, staying on top of my quarterly lab work, and receiving a monthly drug infusion, I adopted a plant-based diet to help reduce the inflammation within my body. It has helped me feel better and function a lot better. Of course, there are times where I get flare-ups regardless of my efforts, but it could be so much worse. There are numerous support groups that I belong to, and I have connected with others who are also in the fight against Lupus.

This is important because Lupus can make you feel alienated, and it is often difficult to explain to others how it feels to live with a chronic illness. The pain is not something that can be seen on the outside so a person can look completely normal to others. Sometimes my body experiences joint and nerve pain so intensely, that all I can do is lay down. Imagine feeling as if your entire body is on fire in different places from head to toe and it continues for days at a time. It is often so much easier to say that I am fine when people ask how I am doing, than to explain my pain.

One thing that I know for sure is that as long as I have breath in my body, I am going to smile. I may have Lupus, but it does not have me. Instead of wondering why I was given this illness, my mindset has changed to making sure that I inspire others to keep going and to NEVER give up.

> *I didn't realize it at the time, but that would become a part of my testimony for how God was the head physician in the operating room on that day.*

Mental health is related to our physical health. A person with good mental health is more likely to contribute more to their physical health. The U.S. Department of Health & Human Services defines it as a person's emotional, social, and psychological sense of well-being. The level of our mental health influences how well we function in various areas of our lives. It affects how well we handle tough times; it impacts our personal relationships with other people as well as how we interact with society.

When we are subjected to times of high stress, chronic illnesses or other traumatic life events, our behaviors, moods, or even self-motivation can be affected. Why? Because often times people who experience these things deal with anxiety and depression. According to the Anxiety and Depression Association of America, approximately 40 million adults deal with one or both, but they can be managed with medication and there is nothing wrong with that. Sometimes the brain needs help with a chemical imbalance. In addition, therapy can also be effective. I used to wonder if either of these things would have helped my mother with her deep-rooted pain. My mental health has surely had its highs and lows. Over the course of my life, I have gone from having feelings of unworthiness, self-loathing, hopelessness, and anxiety, to feeling strong and proud of myself for not giving up regardless of what adversity came my way. For every negative thought that arises, I combat it by reminding myself of what God's word says about me. Almost daily, I look at myself in the mirror and tell myself that I am fearfully and wonderfully made, that I am above and not beneath, and that the peace of God will guard my heart and mind in Christ Jesus. I think we all experience some level of anxiety or even depression at some point in our lives. Maybe you have had moments where all you wanted to do was sleep, or you were feeling sad or worried for no obvious reason. This past year COVID-19 has definitely affected many of us in ways that we would have never imagined. If you find yourself in a place where you need to talk to someone, don't be afraid to do it. Remember, your mental health matters.

> **The level of our mental health influences how well we function in various areas of our lives.**

We all enjoy the occasional meet up with friends or co-workers, whether it is for brunch, dinner, shopping, or just catching a movie. These moments allow us to engage with others, enjoy the change from our usual scenery, and de-stress from the day-to-day challenges of life. This falls under the category of social health which contributes to our overall health, similar to physical and mental health. It explains how well we relate and connect with other people. Social well-being helps to keep stress levels down, which is good for our immune systems and heart health. Having social skills that are well developed is important because that means a person will know how to function in various environments. When we experience a rough patch, it is reassuring to know that there are people whom we can count on to provide the support we need.

Now while we do need to have a healthy social life, there are differences in how social settings affect people. Are you an extrovert or an introvert? Or maybe you fall under the Ambivert term which is a combination of both. People who are extroverted are usually social butterflies, they enjoy entertaining others and tend to feel energized around people. Introverts on the other hand, enjoy the time they get to spend alone. After they have spent time in social settings, they often need to recharge by themselves. Our personality type does not determine how good of a communicator we are or how much we will enjoy ourselves. It just explains how we tend to feel in various settings. No matter where you fall, it is important to understand that what works for someone else may not work for you. Never feel pressured to change in order to try and fit into a certain category or circle of people. We are all uniquely different and that is what makes diversity so beautiful.

You may be saying to yourself, *but I get anxiety when trying to get to know people. Or, I haven't been out in so long that I think I've forgotten how to socialize.* Sometimes there are underlying reasons for why we find it difficult to interact socially. This includes fear of rejection, bad experiences with people, anti-social disorders, autism, or drug use. However, there are things that we can do to improve our social health. Have you ever heard the phrase, "The only way to have a friend is to be one?" Don't be afraid to reach out to someone first. Maybe it's to pay them a compliment or ask their opinion on something. Join different groups that interest you or volunteer. Take the time to learn what healthy relationships look like and cultivate those relationships. After all, these are people who you will want to feel safe in confiding in while knowing they have your back. Know your personal boundaries and go from there. Most importantly, just be yourself!

I have always been an introvert. (Some people would never believe this) I do believe that my early childhood trauma contributed to that. Now I flow with the term Ambivert because I took my power back. I am extremely adventurous, somewhat of an adrenaline junkie. Skydiving, ziplining, and rollercoasters- I love it. (Just don't put me on a Ferris wheel.) I know, it sounds crazy after telling you the other things that I've enjoyed doing but it's the fear of slow heights. Crazy, right? But I have friends that I like to link up with to catch a bite to eat, travel with or do the many things us ladies enjoy doing. I also enjoy my solo time. I have even done solo international travel a few times. It is also refreshing to be able to focus on the stillness and talk to God, read a good book, journal, or just enjoy a good day at home while listening to some good ole throwback or R&B music. It is another form of self-care for me. Even though the joy that I now feel is rather unexplainable, I still think back on where I used to be. I was extremely unapproachable. I held onto the guard that I created many years ago in an effort to keep me safe from people. I realized that the eight-year-old me was now safe. God's got me and He doesn't need any help.

All areas of our health are important. There is no such thing as perfect health, but if we pour into ourselves then we are doing our parts to contribute to a healthy lifestyle. Instead of trying to change everything at one time, make small changes and do not give up if you have a setback. Before you know it, those changes will add up and you will see a difference.

We are all uniquely different and that is what makes diversity so beautiful.

SELF REFLECTIONS

Our level of health impacts our quality of life. Either we are doing things to add to it or doing things to subtract from it. Think about your own health and answer the following questions.

1. **How is your overall health?**

_____
_____
_____

2. **On a scale of 1-10, how important is your health? Why?**

_____
_____
_____
_____

3. **What good habits do you incorporate to promote good health? What are some bad habits that you would like to change?**

_____
_____
_____
_____
_____

4. **Do you have a health goal? Make a list of things that you would like to see manifested in your life.**

_____

_____

_____

_____

_____

_____

_____

_____

_____

_____

_____

_____

_____

_____

_____

_____

Chapter Nine

God's Unwavering Love

The fact that I made it to this chapter is a bit surreal for me. When I started the process of writing this book, it was exciting but also terrifying. I asked myself if I could really do it. Would I be able to reflect on so many difficult areas of my past and stay strong? It was then that I remembered what all of those difficult moments had in common — I survived. Throughout all of the disappointments, failures, heartbreaks, devastating events, feelings of despair and tears shed; I survived it all. Everything that should have destroyed me only made me stronger. I owe all of that to my savior Jesus Christ.

Often times, when we are in the midst of a storm, it is difficult to see anything other than the impact of the storm. My maternal grandmother was named Annie. Gram, as I called her, would always say, "We have to prepare for war in the time of peace." I never understood that statement until I got older; after I went through some things. What I learned was that I had to stay anchored in Christ so that when the enemy threw his fiery darts or created various distractions and tried to plant seeds of doubt in my mind, I would be prepared. Ephesians 6:16 explains that we have to take up the shield of faith in order to extinguish all of the flaming darts of the wicked one. At times, this was easier said than done. Life would be smooth sailing one minute and be full of pits and valleys the next one. You know how it goes; we often have our own plans on how we want to do things but then we are reminded of who is really in control. I feel like God has a sense of humor though and I often imagine Him saying, "let me block this situation right quick because she does not listen!" I will admit that I am very strong willed and sometimes that has worked in my favor. However, that trait has also taught me some life lessons. When I think back on certain moments in my life, I am grateful, grateful that God didn't forget about me even when I seemed to forget about Him.

As I have mentioned, I was brought up in the church. Being born and raised in Florida, my family was Southern Baptist. My father was a Deacon who led Sunday devotion along with his cousin. They would line those old hymns like nobody else could. Many of them I still know today such as, "A Charge to Keep I Have". In my household, it wasn't a Sunday morning if my father didn't put on music by Al Green. He loved the Precious Lord album, especially "The Old Rugged Cross" and "In the Garden" songs. Back in those days, the churches had ceiling fans or A/C window units, so you know the heat could be sweltering at times. It was not uncommon to see the ushers handing out church fans to whomever needed one. The choir would march into the church often singing a spirit-filled song that moved everyone in the congregation. By the time I joined the youth choir, there was no more marching in. However, I do remember how good all of us sounded together! (Shout out to the alto section.) When I think back on those days, it stirs up feelings of nostalgia, but it also makes me think about what my understanding of church was at that time.

My knowledge of what church membership encompassed was limited. I was taught that Jesus loved me, and I should say my prayers every night. During worship you sang and clapped, gave your offering, listened to the good Word, fellowshipped, and went home. When the church had a revival, we were there. We were there for the pastor and the church's anniversary. As I got older and was out of the house, I still attended church, but I started to have questions about God and faith. I noticed all of the unfortunate things that were happening in the world, reflected on things that I'd experienced, thought about the people who I'd personally lost, and I wondered how God could allow these things to happen. I mean, wasn't He omnipotent, omniscient, and omnipresent? Why didn't He stop these tragedies? The uncertainty within me only grew as time went on. I found myself going through the motions of attending church and participating in church activities all the while being somewhat angry with God. If He was the Lord of Lords and King of Kings as my great grandmother always proclaimed, shouldn't my life have been better? Couldn't He have spared me much of the pain that I'd felt throughout my life? I thought that I knew the real reason. It had to be because I was unworthy of His love.

Everything that should have destroyed me only made me stronger.

After all, I was the one whose mother decided to abandon her. I was the one who was targeted and ultimately violated as a child. My grandfather who showered me with unconditional love, praise, and validation, left me alone in this cruel world. So, in my mind there was no way that God could truly love me. As time went on and I became a mother, I repeated the same Sunday routine as I had been taught during my youth. I guess it was just deeply ingrained in me that this is how we were supposed to live our lives. Don't misunderstand what I am saying here. I believed in God; I knew He existed, but my faith wavered due to deep rooted hurt and anger.

There were periods of my life where I stopped attending church regularly. I remember my gram Annie asking me if I had gone to church a few Sundays in a row. My response was that I was either under the weather, had worked a lot, or that I decided to do bedside Baptist. (This is when you sleep in.) I just felt as if there should be more to religion than just the Sunday services, Tuesday night Bible study and revivals. It was during this period that I sought comfort in food, I dated different men while remaining emotionally detached, and eventually I found myself in a dark place. It is always when we are at our lowest point that the enemy really starts messing with us. All it takes is one negative thought deeply planted to take us down the wrong road. Negative seeds/thoughts produce negative results. I knew that it all started in the mind and if I was to win against the attacks, I had to do something different.

Life has a way of bringing us back to where we need to be. My grandma Ruth became chronically ill and although she fought hard, she was unable to win the battle here on earth. I knew that her healing would still happen, but just on the other side of life. After all, she embodied what it meant to be a true disciple of God. Losing people had never been easy for me, much like many of you, I am sure. Although grief is a process that has no specified amount of time for healing, I wasn't prepared for that journey. I had so many memories with her. Who would answer the phone when I called her house? Her tv would no longer be turned to her favorite game shows like *The Price is Right* and *Jeopardy*. The sweet aroma of whatever she was cooking would no longer hit my nose when I entered her house. Yet again, I was faced with feeling abandoned by those that I loved. Of course, I knew that we all have a limited time on earth, but my heart was aching. My heart not only ached for my grandma, but for the love that I always felt with her. I felt as if pieces of me were slowly being picked apart. But I knew that I had to be strong; I had two children who needed me. I could either focus on who was no longer there for me, or I could turn to the One who had never left me.

I began to really think about my life and all that I'd endured. There were moments where I wanted to give up and moments where I even tried, but for some reason I was still here. In the midst of my pain and sadness, God had kept me. Could there be a purpose for my pain? I thought about the countless people in the Bible who had either turned their backs on God or did not believe in Him. Look at Peter for example. After Jesus' arrest, Peter was confronted in the courtyard and accused of being a follower of Jesus. As Jesus had already predicted, Peter denied him three times. Did this disqualify him from being a disciple? Not at all. Jesus saw something in Peter that he could not see in himself. Peter was restored and became a great leader of the disciples. I remember thinking about Paul, the writer of the New Testament. His name was previously Saul, and he did everything he could to destroy the church and any Christians who followed the faith. Saul was also a murderer. While he was heading out on his path to do more harm, he encountered Jesus and his life was changed for the better.

If Jesus accepted these men who had committed some of the most shameful acts, why wouldn't He do the same for me? What I realized was that my shortcomings and failures were not enough to stop God's love for me. His love never ceases, and His mercies never come to an end. Even when I veered off track, He was right there. Regardless of what our past looks like, our age or our current situation, God's grace is sufficient. He has placed something on the inside of both me and you to be used for His glory.

> **All it takes is one negative thought deeply planted to take us down the wrong road.**

After thinking back to all of His grace, I surrendered my heart, mind, soul, and fears to God. It became more about my relationship with my heavenly Father than what religious group I belonged to. When I think about God's promises, I am reassured that there is no problem too great for Him to solve. Often times when we feel weak or incapable of pressing forward, God is waiting on us to call on Him. His strength is perfected in our weakness. Realizing that I did not have to carry the weight of my worries, defeats, and disappointments alone, made me feel free. I finally understood that me, the overseer of so many things in my life, could loosen the grips. Do you know how that felt? Well, it felt amazing do you hear me? I felt as if I had seen the light in more ways than one. The more time that I spent reading God's word and allowed Him to speak to me, I knew without a doubt that I could rely on Him to give me wisdom when I needed it, peace in the midst of my storms, guidance when I felt lost, and so much more. My happiness had bloomed into j-o-y.

So, what is joy? One definition says that it encompasses good cheer and uncontainable happiness. I believe that to be true but the type of joy I experienced was on a deeper level. The type that just lives on the inside of me and cannot be shaken by what happens on the outside. Sure, times get tough, that's a part of life. But the good Word reminds us that pure joy is found in God's presence. I think about how much God loves me and that He gave the ultimate sacrifice of his son Jesus. As a parent, I don't know if I could love another person that much, let alone all of humanity that I would sacrifice my own. It made me think about the immeasurable ways that God had expressed His love for me. He only wanted one thing in return: my whole heart. A heart willing to be open, vulnerable, and selfless. One that was able to share every single part — even the broken, uncertain, and undesirable parts. If you're like me, you may have felt at certain times as if you had done so much wrong that you would never be forgiven. Even though we may fall off the track, our Father still awaits us with open arms; ready to steer us back onto the right one.

I love to read. I always have. It is something so exciting about the feel of a new book in my hand! Whether I am captivated by the title, the cover's design, or my familiarity with the author's work, I know that the words within it will capture my attention. I have lost count of the number in my personal collection, but it is pretty vast. Reading allows me to picture whatever is being conveyed by the author, using my own imagination. I know some people prefer to listen to audio books but it's not my preferred method. There was only one or two books that I recall listening to and those were interesting because of how well the author self-narrated.

My book interests stretch across many genres, one of my favorites being romance. I guess you could say that I am a hopeless romantic as well. I think that we all enjoy the positive effects that love brings. Whether it is the expression of love shared between two people, the love that a grandparent has for their grandchild, or a love for something that we are passionate about, it gives all of the good feels, doesn't it? Similarly, to the love that an author attempts to portray through a romance novel, God's word is a written love story to us. Have you ever written a love letter to someone? I know in these times of texts, emails, and social media, no one really takes the time to write, but think about it. If you wanted to write to someone whom you loved, you would take your time. Every word would be carefully crafted because your goal would be to express how much you cherished that person. A love letter would be an opportunity to pen all of your pinned up emotions, deepest level of intimacy, and true self on paper. Some people aren't the best at verbalizing their feelings and that's okay. Communication occurs in various ways. When I think about the Bible, I feel that God's words are the epitome of true love. He not only spoke about love, but He backed them up with action. His love is available for us all regardless of our race, sex, or culture and there is nothing you nor I can do to change that. Romans 8:38-39 reminds me of that quite often. In essence, it says that nothing can separate us from His love. Not death or life, angels or demons, fears or worries about tomorrow— not even the powers of hell. His love is unstoppable! What the enemy tries to use for evil, God will turn for our good. I am a living witness to that.

Pure joy is found in God's presence.

When I think about my 40 plus years on this earth, I am extremely blessed. Singing – "Couldn't Tell It If I Tried" by the Clark sisters. If you did not know my story, you would never imagine that my early beginnings were not the ideal situation for a young girl to grow and blossom. Throughout my life, there was trauma, pain, unresolved grief, and loss of self. With the amount of devastation that I experienced, I probably should have been eligible for a check as the old people used to say. But GOD! He saw otherwise. He knew that I was destined for greatness before He created me. Every single storm that came my way, prepared me for my purpose. Sometimes we spend an entire lifetime trying to figure out what we are "supposed" to do. The funny thing about that is it's usually already within us but not yet realized. I recently listened to a church sermon and the pastor stated that "Your assignment is in your agitation." That statement summed up everything I'd always felt on the inside of me about helping others without a voice. For as long as I can remember, I have always been a nurturer — deeply bothered by the mistreatment of others. I grew to understand that your job title does not always equate to your passion or your true calling. I am thankful that God has kept me which in turn allowed me to answer the call. What has been knocking at your door and will you answer it? I realized that what was on the inside of me was so important! How could I allow fear to hold me back when it could benefit so may others? I made a choice to do it scared.

I have experienced favor in countless ways. I am a mom to two of the most beautiful gifts in this world which are my son and daughter, and I have some of most supportive people in my life. I have traveled to some of the most breathtaking places and created some unforgettable memories. When the dust settles, what really matters to me are the intangible things that make me who I am. I treasure the small things, things we often take for granted. As you go about your day, smile a little more, be kind to a stranger, show love to one another. You never know who needs it.

I don't know what lead you to purchase my book, but I am very thankful for your support. I hope that it left you with some nuggets that you can apply as you navigate throughout your life's journey or the life of someone else you encounter along the way. While I spent many of my years feeling misunderstood, unaccepted, and unworthy, I now have a peace that no one can take away from me. For every negative thought that arises, God's promises are evidence of just the opposite. I encourage you to live your life out loud. You may be thinking, well what does she mean by that? Listen, we only get one life to live. Do what you have always dreamt of doing. Step out on faith even when fear tries to tell you that you can't do it. Be bold! Inspire others! Make more deposits into someone's life than you withdraw. Find your joy. I can honestly say that today I am no longer bound by my past. No more shame, blame, insecurity, pain or unforgiveness. The shackles are gone. I have outgrown the confinement of my mind and the thoughts that told me I would not make it.

I have outgrown my cocoon and just like the butterfly, I am free.

Available Resources

American Foundation for Suicide Prevention
800-273-8255
https://afsp.org/

Substance Abuse and Mental Health Services Administration
800-662-HELP
https://www.samhsa.gov/find-help/national-helpline

Rape, Abuse & Incest National Network (RAINN)
800-656-HOPE
https://www.rainn.org/about-rainn

National Child Abuse Coalition
800-4-A-Child
https://nationalchildabusecoalition.org/

National Domestic Violence Hotline
800-799-7233
https://www.thehotline.org/

References

Achauer, Hilary. "Why You Need to Put Yourself First and How to Do It". Whole Life Challenge. Retrieved from: https://www.wholelifechallenge.com/why-you-need-to-put-yourself-first-and-how-to-do-it/

American Psychological Association. 2019. "Making stepfamilies work". Retrieved from: https://www.apa.org/topics/stepfamily

Anxiety & Depression Association of America. 2021. "Facts & Statistics". ADAA. Retrieved from: https://adaa.org/about-adaa/press-room/facts-statistics

Beresin, Eugene. 2019, August 7. "Why Chores Are Important for Kids". Psychology Today. Retrieved from: https://www.psychologytoday.com/us/blog/inside-out-outside-in/201908/why-chores-are-important-kids

Burton, Krista. 2019. "Top Ways to Relax in the City". Monq. Retrieved from: https://monq.com/eo/destress-relaxation/ways-relax-city/

Center for Disease Control and Prevention. "Preventing Child Sexual Abuse". Retrieved from: www.cdc.gov

Children's Health. 2021. "The Importance of Life Balance for Kids". Retrieved from: https://www.childrens.com/health-wellness/help-your-child-find-balance

Deep Soulful Love. 2020, Apr. 27. "How To Overcome Fear of Abandonment". Retrieved from: https://deepsoulfullove.com/how-to-overcome-fear-of-abandonment/

Fallon, Cara Kiernan and Karlawish, Jason. 2019, July 17. "It's Time to Change the Definition of Health". Stat. Retrieved from: https://www.statnews.com/2019/07/17/change-definition-health/

Felman, Adam. 2020, April 19. "What is Good Health". Medical News Today. Retrieved from: https://www.medicalnewstoday.com/articles/150999#types

Gibson, Aaliyah. 2020, August 4. "Parenting Mistakes: Offensive Things Damaging Your Relationship with Your Child". The Active Times. Retrieved from: https://www.theactivetimes.com/home/didnt-realize-offending-children

Gordon, Sherry. 2020, September 17. "What Is Emotional Abuse". Very Well Mind. Retrieved from: https://www.verywellmind.com/identify-and-cope-with-emotional-abuse-4156673

Jacobson, Sheri. 2016, June 2. "Abandonment Issues-Are They Your Real Issue". Harley Therapy. Retrieved from: https://www.harleytherapy.co.uk/counselling/abandonment-issues.htm

Kohli, Sahaj. 2016, May 20. "14 Common Misconceptions About People Who Go to Therapy". HuffPost. Retrieved from: https://www.huffpost.com/entry/misconceptions-about-therapy_b_7286

Lancer, Darlene. 2017, October 29. "Are You Being Emotionally Abandoned?" Psychology Today. Retrieved from: https://www.psychologytoday.com/us/blog/toxic-relationships/201710/are-you-being-emotionally-abandoned

Lancer, Darlene. 2017, June 6. "The Truth About Abusers and What to Do". Psychology Today. Retrieved from: https://www.psychologytoday.com/us/blog/toxic-relationships/201706/the-truth-about-abusers-abuse-and-what-do

Martin, Sharon. 2018, December 21. "Why We Abandon Ourselves and How to Stop". PsychCentral. Retrieved from: https://psychcentral.com/blog/imperfect/2018/12/why-we-abandon-ourselves-and-how-to-stop

Mayo Clinic. 2020. "Stepfamilies: How to help your child adjust". Retrieved from: https://www.mayoclinic.org/healthy-lifestyle/childrens-health/in-depth/stepfamilies/art-20047046

Mendel, Betsy. 2017, April 13. "7 steps to making your health your No. 1 priority". Los Angeles Times. Retrieved from: https://www.latimes.com/health/la-he-resolutions-versus-commitments-20170408-story.html

Mind Your Mind. 2021. "Get Ready for Your Appointment". Retrieved from: https://mindyourmind.ca/help/get-ready-your-appointment

Pennsylvania Coalition Against Rape, "Learn Examples of Child Sexual Abuse". PCAR. Retrieved from: https://pcar.org/learn-examples-of-child-sexual-abuse

Pietrangelo, Ann. 2018, December 6. "How to Recognize the Signs of Mental and Emotional Abuse". Healthline. Retrieved from: https://www.healthline.com/health/signs-of-mental-abuse

Pietrangelo, Ann. 2019, March 29. "Ways to Begin Recovery". Healthline. Retrieved from: https://www.healthline.com/health/mental-health/effects-of-emotional-abuse#ways-to-begin-recovery

Richo, David. 2020, September 30. "13 Strategies to Deal with Your Emotional Triggers". Experience Life. Lifetime. Retrieved from: https://experiencelife.com/article/13-strategies-to-deal-with-your-emotional-triggers/

Shaikh, Atiba. 2015. "How to Maintain Peace and Joy Despite Your Everyday Struggles". Blog Tiny Buddha. Retrieved from: https://tinybuddha.com/blog/how-to-maintain-peace-and-joy-despite-your-everyday-struggles/

Skilled at Life. 2018. "Why Hobbies Are Important". Retrieved from: www.skilledatlife.com/why-hobbies-are-important/

T., Buddy. 2020. "Signs That Indicate a Relationship Could Turn Violent". Very Well Mind. Retrieved from: https://www.verywellmind.com/signs-that-a-relationship-could-turn-violent-4100203

The Rape Crisis Center. 2021. "Statistics". Retrieved from: https://rapecrisis.com/statistics/

Tracy, Natasha. 2012, July 24. "Emotionally Abusive Men and Women: Who Are They". Healthy Place. Retrieved from: https://www.healthyplace.com/abuse/emotional-psychological-abuse/emotionally-abusive-men-and-women-who-are-they

Withers, Randy. 2018, January 17. "Here Are 5 Unbelievably Toxic Things Good Parents Never Do". Mission. Retrieved from: https://medium.com/the-mission/here-are-5-unbelievably-toxic-things-good-parents-never-do-1fc3477657c

About the Author

Monaye Etana, a native Floridian, is a finance professional, mentor, and a certified Grief Recovery Specialist. She is the owner of The Grief Path and runs a Lupus blog to inspire others on a similar journey. Monaye is also the proud mom of her son Tony and her daughter Kaelyn. For more information about Monaye, you can visit: www.favoredandfree.com. You may also follow her on Instagram @unbreakable_survivher and @thegriefpath.